Y0-BYU-294

## Function Keys

| Function Key | Key Name |
| --- | --- |
| F1 | Help |
| F2 | Do-It! |
| Alt–F2 | Show SQL |
| F3 | Up Image |
| Alt–F3 | Instant Script Record Toggle |
| F4 | Down Image |
| Alt–F4 | Instant Script Play |
| F5 | Example |
| Alt–F5 | Field View |
| F6 | Check |
| Alt–F6 | Check Plus |
| Ctrl–F6 | Check Descending |
| Shift–F6 | Group |
| F7 | Form Toggle |
| Alt–F7 | Instant Report |
| Ctrl–F7 | Graph |
| F8 | Clear Image |
| Alt–F8 | Clear All |
| F9 | Edit |
| Alt–F9 | CoEdit |
| F10 | Menu |
| Ctrl–F10 | Quattro Pro |

# Computer users are not all alike.
# Neither are SYBEX books.

We know our customers have a variety of needs. They've told us so. And because we've listened, we've developed several distinct types of books to meet the needs of each of our customers. What are you looking for in computer help?

If you're looking for the basics, try the **ABC's** series, or for a more visual approach, select **Teach Yourself**.

**Mastering** and **Understanding** titles offer you a step-by-step introduction, plus an in-depth examination of intermediate-level features, to use as you progress.

Our **Up & Running** series is designed for computer-literate consumers who want a no-nonsense overview of new programs. Just 20 basic lessons, and you're on your way.

SYBEX **Encyclopedias** provide a *comprehensive reference* and explanation of all of the commands, features and functions of the subject software.

Sometimes a subject requires a special treatment that our standard series doesn't provide. So you'll find we have titles like **Advanced Techniques, Handbooks, Tips & Tricks**, and others that are specifically tailored to satisfy a unique need.

You'll find SYBEX publishes a variety of books on every popular software package. Looking for computer help? Help Yourself to SYBEX.

## For a complete catalog of our publications:

SYBEX Inc.
2021 Challenger Drive, Alameda, CA 94501
Tel: (415) 523-8233/(800) 227-2346 Telex: 336311
Fax: (415) 523-2373

*SYBEX is committed to using natural resources wisely to preserve and improve our environment. This is why we have been printing the text of books like this one on recycled paper since 1982.*

*This year our use of recycled paper will result in the saving of more than 15,300 trees. We will lower air pollution effluents by 54,000 pounds, save 6,300,000 gallons of water, and reduce landfill by 2,700 cubic yards.*

*In choosing a SYBEX book you are not only making a choice for the best in skills and information, you are also choosing to enhance the quality of life for all of us.*

# Paradox 3.5
# User's Instant Reference

# Paradox® 3.5
# User's Instant Reference

*Loy Anderson, Ph.D.*

*Cary Jensen, Ph.D.*

SYBEX ®

San Francisco • Paris • Düsseldorf • Soest

Acquisitions Editor: Dianne King
Developmental Editor: James A. Compton
Editor: Stefan Grünwedel
Technical Editor: Charlie Russel
Word Processors: Scott Campbell, Ann Dunn, Deborah Maizels, Lisa Mitchell
Series Book Designer: Ingrid Owen
Screen Graphics: Cuong Le
Desktop Publishing Production: Len Gilbert
Proofreader: Lisa Haden
Cover Designer: Archer Design
Screen reproductions produced by XenoFont.
XenoFont is a trademark of XenoSoft.

Library of Congress Card Number: 90-71676
ISBN: 0-89588-766-5
Manufactured in the United States of America
10 9 8 7 6 5 4 3 2 1

# SYBEX INSTANT REFERENCES

We've designed SYBEX *Instant References* to meet the evolving needs of software users, who want essential information easily accessible, in a clear and concise form. Our best authors have distilled their expertise into compact reference guides in which you can look up the precise steps for using any feature, including the available options. More than just summaries, these books also provide insights into effective usage drawn from our authors' wealth of experience.

Other SYBEX *Instant References* are:

*AutoCAD Instant Reference*
George Omura

*dBASE IV 1.1 Programmer's Instant Reference*
Alan Simpson

*dBASE IV 1.1 User's Instant Reference*
Alan Simpson

*DOS Instant Reference*
Greg Harvey and
Kay Yarborough Nelson

*Harvard Graphics Instant Reference*
Gerald Jones

*Lotus 1-2-3 Instant Reference, Release 2.2*
Greg Harvey and
Kay Yarborough Nelson

*Norton Utilities Instant Reference*
Michael Gross

*PC Tools Deluxe 6 Instant Reference*
Gordon McComb

*WordPerfect 5 Instant Reference*
Greg Harvey and
Kay Yarborough Nelson

*WordPerfect 5.1 Instant Reference*
Greg Harvey and
Kay Yarborough Nelson

*To Bart Anderson*

# Acknowledgments

We want to thank the fine people at SYBEX for their hard work on this book. Notably, Dr. R.S. Langer and Dianne King for making this project a reality; Jim Compton, our developmental editor, for his support and guidance; Stefan Grünwedel for his skillful editing; Charlie Russel for his thorough technical review; Michael Gross for his production assistance; and to the many others at SYBEX who were involved in this project. We also want to thank Nan Borreson at Borland International for her valuable encouragement and assistance, as well as the helpful technical support people at Borland.

# *Table of Contents*

## *Chapter Three*
## VIEWING AND EDITING TABLES

## *Chapter Four*
## DESIGNING FORMS

## *Chapter Five*

## DESIGNING REPORTS

## Chapter Six

### QUERIES

## Chapter Seven

### CREATING CROSSTABS AND GRAPHS

## Chapter Eight

### PARADOX TOOLS

*Chapter Nine*

## SCRIPTS

*Chapter Ten*

## PARADOX ON A NETWORK

# *Introduction*

This book covers all the major features of Paradox 3.0 and 3.5 in a
concise manner so you can easily look up how to do a particular
task. We assume that you will be using this reference book while
you are working with the software. With this in mind, we have kept
the entries in this book short, describing only the essential information to instruct or refresh you on specific tasks. If you are a new
Paradox user, or are currently using a database application written
in the Paradox Application Language (PAL), this book can provide
a quick way for you to learn more about Paradox.

## ABOUT VERSION 3.5

Paradox 3.5 is nearly identical to version 3.0. The most important
addition to version 3.5 is in how Paradox manages your computer's
memory resources. With the addition of VROOMM (Virtual Real-
time Object-Oriented Memory Management) technology, Paradox
requires less memory to run—so it runs faster than ever. Paradox
3.5 also includes Turbo Drive, a DOS extender. Turbo Drive allows
Paradox to use extended memory (up to 16 MB of RAM) on 80286-
based (and higher) computers. In addition, VROOMM with Turbo
Drive allows Paradox to manage any expanded or extended
memory available, adjusting its memory use as required. (Paradox
3.5 officially replaces Paradox 386.)

Other improvements to Paradox 3.5 include:

- The availability of PAL variables and some functions in
  reports and forms (see Appendix A)

- Greater connectivity to Borland's spreadsheet program,
  Quattro Pro version 2.0

- Access through the separate product Paradox SQL Link to
  data on database servers (see Appendix B)

- Nine linked tables in forms and reports (only five are allowed in version 3.0)

# HOW TO USE THIS BOOK

This book is organized functionally so you can locate related topics within a single chapter. The entries are intended to provide you with the essential information about Paradox features. Each entry begins with the specific steps required to perform an operation so you can quickly accomplish it. This is followed by a description of what the feature is for and a list of options and additional notes. References to related topics are also given.

When a series of menu selections must be made to perform an operation, they are listed one after another, without punctuation. For example:

Tools More Directory

indicates that you should first select Tools, then More, then Directory.

Words or characters that you must type in *exactly* are printed in **boldface.** For example, **PARADOX** is the command you enter to start Paradox from the DOS prompt.

## Chapter One
# PARADOX BASICS

This chapter describes how to start Paradox and navigate through its menu system. We assume that Paradox is already installed on your computer. If it is not, refer to a book such as Alan Simpson's *Mastering Paradox* (SYBEX, 1990) for instructions.

# STARTING PARADOX

Besides the basic start-up procedure, there are two variations on getting Paradox up and running: by specifying command-line options and loading a script simultaneously.

## To Perform a Basic Start-Up

1. Go to the DOS prompt (usually C:).

2. Type **PARADOX** and press Enter. (Type **PARADOX3** if you are using Paradox version 3.0.)

## To Specify a Command-Line Option

Type **PARADOX option1 option2...** at the DOS prompt and press Enter.

**What For?** To customize some features of your Paradox session. For instance, to run Paradox with black-and-white menus and screens, type **PARADOX -B&W**. Options must be separated by at least one space. Table 1.1 contains a list of the available options and their uses.

## To Load a Script Simultaneously

• Type **PARADOX scriptname** at the DOS prompt and press Enter. Make sure that *scriptname* resides in the current directory

Or

• Simply name the script INIT.SC. Upon loading, Paradox automatically executes any script called INIT.SC if it is stored in your private Paradox directory

**What For?** To have Paradox run a script as soon as the program is loaded. This is useful when you want to run an application written in PAL (Paradox Application Language) immediately upon loading

**Table 1.1:** Command-Line Options

| OPTION | PARADOX VERSION(S) | USE |
|--------|-------------------|-----|
| –B&W | 3.0, 3.5 | Displays screen in monochrome |
| –CACHEK [NUM] | 3.5 | Indicates the size (in kilobytes) of the cache |
| –COLOR | 3.0, 3.5 | Indicates you are using a color monitor and graphics adapter, if you have changed either since installing Paradox |
| –EMK [NUM] | 3.0, 3.5 | Allocates less than all the available expanded memory to Paradox |
| –EXTK [NUM] | 3.5 | Allocates less than all the available extended memory to Paradox |
| –MONO | 3.0, 3.5 | Indicates you are using a monochrome monitor and graphics adapter, if you have changed either since installing Paradox |
| –NET [PATH] | 3.0, 3.5 | Defines an alternate path for the PARADOX.NET file |
| –PROT | 3.5 | Runs Paradox in protected mode |

**Table 1.1:** Command-Line Options (continued)

| OPTION | PARADOX VERSION(S) | USE |
|---|---|---|
| –QPRO | 3.5 | Establishes a link to Quattro Pro, v.2; Paradox must be in protected mode for this to work |
| –REAL | 3.5 | Runs Paradox in real mode |
| –SHARE | 3.0, 3.5 | Operates Paradox in a network environment when you are connected to a non-dedicated server or are simulating a network environment on a single multitasking computer |
| –SNOW | 3.0, 3.5 | With a CGA, eliminates or reduces interference in the display |
| –SQL ON *or* –SQL OFF | 3.5 | Activates (on) or does not activate (off) an installed SQL link |
| –STACK [N] | 3.5 | Specifies the size of the internal stack (8–64K) for use with PAL programs |

**Table 1.1:** Command-Line Options (continued)

| OPTION | PARADOX VERSION(S) | USE |
|---|---|---|
| –TABLEK [N] | 3.5 | Specifies the minimum memory allocated (in kilobytes) for table buffers |
| –USER [NAME] | 3.0, 3.5 | Defines your user name when using Paradox on a network |

Paradox. To do this, add the name of the script you want to execute after you type **PARADOX**. Be sure that this script is in the current directory.

● **NOTE** While Paradox is loading, it reads your Paradox configuration to determine specific characteristics for your Paradox session, including the screen colors and the default printer setup. You define these characteristics with the Paradox Custom Configuration Program (mentioned in this chapter).

# THE MAIN MENU

The Main menu is displayed across the top of the screen. Below is a description of its options:

**View:** Views a table

**Ask:** Queries one or more tables

**Report:** Designs, changes, or prints a report

**Create:** Creates a table

**Modify:** Edits, coedits, or sorts data in a table; restructures a table

**Image:** Changes the display characteristics of a table; creates a Crosstab table or graph

**Forms:** Designs or changes a form

**Tools:** Changes, copies, renames, or deletes a Paradox object; imports or exports data; requests information about (or modifies) the Paradox environment

**Scripts:** Plays, records, or changes a script

**Help:** Accesses the help system

**Exit:** Leaves Paradox

# THE WORKSPACE AND IMAGES

• **DEFINITION**    You can think of the *workspace* as the place where you work with Paradox tables, forms, and queries. Visually, the workspace is represented by the space between the menu and the bottom of the screen, although it actually extends beyond the confines of the screen.

An *image* is a displayed table on the workspace. An image can be viewed in either table view (viewing an actual table image), form view (viewing the data in the table through a form), or as a query form. You can display more than one image on the workspace at once. The last image you add to the workspace will be the *current* image, i.e., the image in which the cursor is active.

## To Move among Multiple Images on the Workspace

- Press F3 (Up Image) to move the cursor up one image

- Press F4 (Down Image) to move the cursor down one image

**What For?**    To make an image active when there is more than one image on the workspace. (You can't work in an image unless it is active.)

● **NOTE**    Each image displayed on the workspace reduces the amount of memory available to Paradox by at least 2K. Therefore, it is always good practice to remove an image from the workspace with the F8 (Clear Image) key when you no longer need it.

# SYSTEM MODES

Paradox's 12 system modes are shown in Table 1.2. They represent the different functional areas in which you perform different tasks. (Paradox displays the mode under which you are currently operating at the top right of the screen—except for the Main mode.)

When you start Paradox, you are in the Main mode.

## To Enter System Modes

Make the corresponding menu selections shown in Table 1.2.

**See Also**    Table 1.4 for shortcuts to some system modes.

## To Return to the Main Mode

1.    Press F10 (Menu) to display the menu for the mode under which you are currently working.

2.    Decide to do one of the following:

   •    Select DO-IT! from the displayed menu or press F2 (Do-It!) to save any operations or modifications you were performing

   •    Select Cancel from the displayed menu to cancel any operations or modifications you were performing Paradox asks you to confirm the cancel request.

Select Yes to confirm the cancellation and return to the Main menu or No to return the cursor to the workspace

**Table 1.2**: System Modes

| MODE | MENU SELECTIONS |
|------|-----------------|
| CoEdit | Modify CoEdit |
| Create | Create |
| DataEntry | Modify DataEntry *or* Modify MultiEntry |
| Edit | Modify Edit |
| Forms | Forms Design *or* Forms Change |
| Graph | Image Graph Modify |
| Main | *Default* |
| Password | Tools More Protect Password Table |
| Report | Report Design *or* Report Change |
| Restructure | Modify Restructure |
| Script | Scripts Editor Edit *or* Scripts Editor Write |
| Sort | Modify Sort |

**Note:** *Make these menu selections from the Main mode*

# SELECTING FROM MENUS

Most of Paradox's features are accessed through menus. (The rest are selected with function keys, also described in this chapter.) Before you can use a menu, it must be activated. A menu is active only when it is displayed. (If the cursor appears in an image, the menu is not displayed and is, therefore, inactive.)

## To Display a Menu

Press F10 (Menu).

Paradox displays the menu appropriate for the current system mode, and moves the cursor to the first menu option and highlights it. A description of it also appears on the line below. You can change which menu option is highlighted by using the keys listed in Table 1.3.

**Table 1.3:** Keys for Moving Around Menus

| KEY | EFFECT |
|-----|--------|
| Ctrl– ← | Moves one screenful of menu options to the left |
| Ctrl– → | Moves one screenful of menu options to the right |
| End | Moves to the last menu option |
| Enter | Selects highlighted menu option |
| Esc | Returns cursor to the workspace (if you were previously working in the workspace) or to the previous menu (if you are viewing a submenu) |
| Home | Moves to the first menu option |
| ← | Moves cursor one menu option to the left |
| → | Moves cursor one menu option to the right |

## To Select Menu Options

- Use the keys shown in Table 1.3 to highlight a menu option and press Enter

Or

- Press the first letter of the desired menu option name. If other option names share that letter, Paradox will display a shorter menu that lists just them. You can then use the keys shown in Table 1.3 to select the menu option you want. Alternatively, you can just keep typing in the name of the option until the menu of similarly named options narrows to the one you want

In many cases, when you select a menu option, Paradox will display another menu from which you can select other options.

## To Return to a Menu from a Submenu

Press the Esc (Escape) key. (Press it more than once if you're in a nested submenu.)

# FUNCTION KEYS

The function keys used in Paradox are shown in Table 1.4. Some of them provide a second, and typically quicker, way to access the same features that can be accessed through making menu selections.

**Table 1.4:** Function Keys

| FUNCTION KEY | KEY NAME | EFFECT |
|---|---|---|
| F1 | Help | Accesses the help system |
| F2 | Do-It! | Executes the command |

**Table 1.4:** Function Keys (continued)

| FUNCTION KEY | KEY NAME | EFFECT |
|---|---|---|
| Alt–F2 | Show SQL | Shows SQL statements generated by Paradox based on a query of database server tables |
| F3 | Up Image | When multiple images are present in the workspace, moves the cursor up one image, making that image current |
| Alt–F3 | Instant Script Record | Starts and stops recording an instant script |
| F4 | Down Image | When multiple images are present in the workspace, moves the cursor down one image, making that image current |
| Alt–F4 | Instant Script Play | Plays an instant script |
| F5 | Example | In a query image, indicates that the next characters you type in a field are an example |
| Alt–F5 | Field View | Enters field view |

**Table 1.4**: Function Keys (continued)

| FUNCTION KEY | KEY NAME | EFFECT |
|---|---|---|
| F6 | Check | Places a ✓ in a field of a query to include unique values from the field in the Answer table and sort them in ascending order |
| Alt-F6 | Check Plus | Places a ✓+ in a field of a query to include all values from the field in the Answer table, but not to sort them |
| Ctrl–F6 | Check Descending | Places a ✓▼ in a field of a query to include unique values from the field in the Answer table and sort them in descending order |
| Shift–F6 | Group | Defines a group in a set query without including the field in the Answer table |
| F7 | Form Toggle | Toggles between table view and form view of a table |
| Alt–F7 | Instant Report | Produces the standard report of the current table |
| Ctrl–F7 | Graph | Produces a graph based on the current table |

**Table 1.4:** Function Keys (continued)

| FUNCTION KEY | KEY NAME | EFFECT |
|---|---|---|
| F8 | Clear Image | Removes the current image from the workspace |
| Alt–F8 | Clear All | Removes all images from the workspace |
| F9 | Edit | Enters Edit mode when at least one image is on the workspace |
| Alt–F9 | CoEdit | Enters CoEdit mode when at least one image is on the workspace |
| F10 | Menu | Displays the primary menu for the current system mode and activates the cursor in the menu |
| Ctrl–F10 | Quattro Pro | Switches to Quattro Pro (requires use of the –QPRO command-line option) |

# KEY COMBINATIONS

Paradox provides a number of key combinations that allow you to access a particular feature quickly. They are listed in Table 1.5.

**Table 1.5:** Key Combinations

| KEY COMBINATION | KEY NAME | EFFECT |
|---|---|---|
| Alt–K | Key Viol | During a CoEdit session, toggles between an existing record in a table and a new record with a conflicting key |
| Alt–L | Lock Toggle | Locks or unlocks a record |
| Alt–O | Big DOS | Exits temporarily to DOS |
| Alt–R | Refresh | Updates the screen (while using Paradox in a multi-user environment) |
| Alt–Z | Zoom Next | Moves to the next occurrence of a specified field value after first using Ctrl–Z (Zoom) |
| Ctrl–Backspace | | Erases contents of entire field |
| Ctrl–Break | | Stops the processing of a script or query or stops displaying a report |
| Ctrl–D | Ditto | Copies value from same field of the previous record in a table |
| Ctrl–F | Field View | Enters field view for the current field and record in a table |

**Table 1.5:** Key Combinations (continued)

| KEY COMBINATION | KEY NAME | EFFECT |
|---|---|---|
| Ctrl– ← | | Moves the cursor one screenful of fields to the left in a table or query image |
| Ctrl–O | Little DOS | Exits temporarily to DOS (with less memory available than using Alt–O) |
| Ctrl–R | Rotate | Rotates current field in a table or query image |
| Ctrl– → | | Moves the cursor one screenful of fields to the left in a table or query image |
| Ctrl–U | Undo | Undoes the last change made to a table during an editing session |
| Ctrl–X | Crosstab | Produces a crosstab based on the current table |
| Ctrl–Y | Delete Line | Deletes text left of the cursor in a report |
| Ctrl–Z | Zoom | Moves to a specified field value or pattern in a table |

# USING THE HELP SYSTEM

## To Get Help

Press the F1 (Help) key.

**What For?** To display a help screen similar to the one shown in Figure 1.1 at any time during your Paradox session. This feature is context sensitive, meaning that you'll see a help screen with information specific to the mode in which you are currently working. Additional topics are listed in the Help menu at the top. Select any of these to display additional information.

## To Clear a Help Screen

Select Paradox from the Help menu or press the Esc key.

## To See the Help Index

1.  Press F1 (Help) to access the help system.

2.  Press F1 (Help) again.

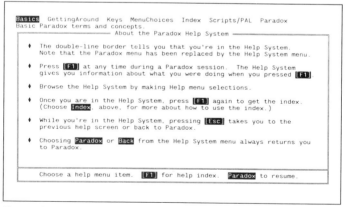

**Figure 1.1:** The help index

**What For?**   To locate information about a feature that was not described in the first help screen. The help index is shown in Figure 1.2. It contains an alphabetical listing of most Paradox commands, modes, features, and functions. You can use the cursor keys to highlight your topic of interest and then press Enter to display that information. You can also search through the topics with Ctrl–Z (Zoom) and Alt–Z (Zoom Next).

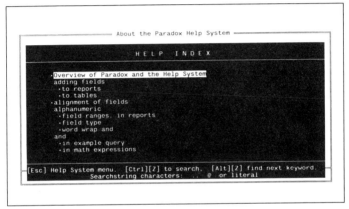

**Figure 1.2:** The help index

# THE CUSTOM CONFIGURATION PROGRAM

There are many parameters of the Paradox program that you can customize to meet your specific needs. These include how Paradox treats blank values in tables, the default printer settings, and the colors used for displaying Paradox screens. All of these parameters, and more, can be changed with the Custom Configuration Program (CCP). The CCP is a script that you either play from within Paradox or specify after the PARADOX command when you first start Paradox from the DOS prompt. The CCP looks and operates very much like Paradox itself: you select options from the displayed menus to configure the system the way you want.

## To Use the Custom Configuration Program

1.  From the main mode, press F10 (Menu) and select Scripts Play.

2.  If Custom is in the current directory, type **CUSTOM** or press Enter and select Custom from the menu of scripts on the current directory. If the Custom program is not in the current directory, type **CUSTOM** and include the directory path.

3.  Select the parameters you want for your Paradox session and change them as you wish.

4.  When you are through customizing the configuration, press F2 (Do-It!) to save your changes. Paradox will ask you to indicate where the configuration information should be stored.

5.  Select Harddisk if you are running Paradox on a stand-alone PC. If you are running Paradox on a network, select Network and confirm the path of the configuration file.

# EXITING PARADOX

## To Exit Paradox

1.  From the main mode, press F10 (Menu) and select Exit. Paradox will prompt you to confirm your request to exit.

2.  Select Yes to exit or No to return to Paradox.

● **NOTE**   When you exit, Paradox checks and closes all tables, and deletes all temporary tables you were working on during your session. If you want to save the data in any temporary tables, you must rename the temporary tables before exiting Paradox.

## Chapter Two

# CREATING AND
# RESTRUCTURING TABLES

In Paradox, your data are stored in tables. A table consists of rows, called *records*, and columns, called *fields*. When you create a table, you must tell Paradox how many fields, and of what type, the table is to contain. This is called the table's *structure*. (The number of records depends on how many data you have.)

This chapter shows you how to create a table and restructure an existing one.

# TABLE PARAMETERS

Paradox tables can hold a maximum of 255 fields, of which there are five types: alphanumeric, numeric, short numeric, currency, and date. The maximum size of a single record is 4000 characters. If your table is keyed (indexed), however, the maximum size of a single record cannot be more than 1350 characters. The size of a table cannot exceed 256 megabytes; thus, the maximum number of records a table could hold is close to 256 million. However, Paradox tables containing more than 200,000 records are quite rare.

**See Also** *Field Names and Types* and *Key Fields and Keyed Tables* (this chapter).

# TABLE NAMES

When you create a table in Paradox, you must name it. This name will be used for all members of the table's family (e.g., forms and reports associated with the table), although the file extensions assigned to them will differ. (The extension for the table proper is .DB.) A table name can contain up to eight characters, and must consist of letters, numbers, or the special characters !, @, #, $, %, &, (, ), −, _ , {, }, ~, ', or `. A table name cannot include spaces. Two tables in the same directory cannot carry the same name.

## TEMPORARY TABLES

There are 12 special tables used by Paradox, called *temporary tables*. Table 2.1 lists the 12 tables and the contents of each.

• **NOTE** Certain operations, such as performing a query, result in the automatic creation of one or more temporary tables. If you give your table the name of one of these temporary tables and then perform the operation, Paradox will replace your table with the one it automatically creates. Moreover, whenever you change directories or exit the system, Paradox automatically erases any tables that have a temporary-table name. So avoid giving your table one of these special names.

**Table 2.1:** Temporary Tables

| TABLE NAME | CONTENTS |
|---|---|
| Answer | Results of a query |
| Changed | Records that are changed in a query |
| Crosstab | Results of a crosstab |
| Deleted | Records that are deleted in a delete query |
| Entry | New records created when you use the DataEntry or MultiEntry option |
| Family | A list of a table's family |
| Inserted | Records that are inserted in an insert query |
| Keyviol | Duplicate records from a keyed table |
| List | List of tables, scripts, table locks, user names, or files |
| Password | List of auxiliary passwords |
| Problems | Records that have problems after a table is restructured |
| Struct | Structure of a table |

# CREATING A TABLE

Creating a table in Paradox involves providing a name for it and defining its structure.

## To Create a Table

1. Press F10 (Menu) from the Main mode and select Create.

2. Enter a valid table name. (See *Table Names*, this chapter.) Paradox will place you in the Create mode and display the table called Struct shown in Figure 2.1.

3. Enter the name of your table's first field and its field type in the first row of Struct. (See *Field Names and Types*, this chapter.)

4. Enter the name of the second field and its field type in the second row of Struct, and so on.

5. When you are through entering the structure of your new table, press F2 (Do-It!).

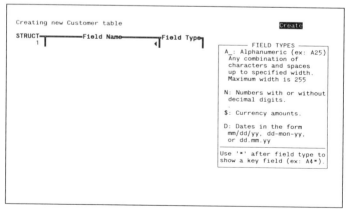

**Figure 2.1:** The Struct table

## To Display the Create (or Restructure) Menu

Press F10 (Menu) while in the Create (or Restructure) mode. (See *Restructuring a Table*, this chapter.)

Both menus have the following options:

**Borrow:** Borrows the structure of another table

**Help:** Accesses the help system (same as pressing F1)

**DO-IT!:** Creates or restructures a table using the defined structure (same as pressing F2)

**Cancel:** Cancels the creation or restructuring of a table and returns you to the workspace

## To Borrow Another Table's Structure

1. Press F10 (Menu) from the Create (or Restructure) mode and select Borrow.

2. Enter the name of the table whose structure you want to borrow, or press Enter and select from a menu of tables in the current directory.

3. Press F2 (Do-It!) or press F10 (Menu) and select DO-IT!.

**What For?**  This technique allows you to create several tables that share the same structure. When you borrow the structure of another table, it is entered into the Struct table below the position of the cursor.

# FIELD NAMES AND TYPES

Field names can contain up to 25 characters and each name must be unique, regardless of how you capitalize letters. Field names may consist of letters, numbers, and spaces, although they cannot begin with a space. They may also contain any other printable keyboard characters, *except* the following:  [, ], (, ), {, }, ", the combination –>, or the # character alone.

There are five valid field types: alphanumeric, numeric, short numeric, currency, and date.

**Alphanumeric** fields are used to hold text, such as a name, address, and description. You define one by placing an *A* followed by the size of the field (in number of characters) in the Field Type column of the Struct table. For example, if you define a field as A20, the field could contain up to 20 characters. The maximum size of an alphanumeric field is 255 characters.

**Numeric** is the standard field type for storing numbers, which can be up to 15 digits long, including decimal places. Values with more than 15 digits are expressed in scientific notation. Numbers can range from $\pm 10^{-308}$ to $\pm 10^{308}$. Define a field as numeric by entering a capital *N* in the Field Type column of the Struct table.

**Short numeric** fields are appropriate when data are only *integers* from −32,768 to 32,767. To define a field as short numeric, enter a capital *S* in the Field Type column of the Struct table.

**Currency** fields have the same characteristics as numeric fields, but are displayed differently when in table view, form view, or the default report-format. To define a currency field, enter the $ character in the Field Type column of the Struct table.

**Date** fields are used to hold dates between 1 January 100 and 31 December 9999. Dates can be entered in one of three formats (MM/DD/YY, DD-MMM-YY, or DD.MM.YY) and can include a two-digit (20th century only) or four-digit year. Specify a date field by placing a capital *D* in the Field Type column of the Struct table.

# KEY FIELDS AND KEYED TABLES

You can define one or more fields in a table as a *key field*. All key fields in a table must appear in the first field positions of the Struct table *before* any unkeyed fields.

A table containing one or more key fields is referred to as a *keyed table*. A keyed table has three main characteristics: records are sorted by the values in the key field(s); each record must be unique, based on the values in the key field(s); and certain Paradox operations are performed substantially faster than on unkeyed tables.

## To Key a Field

1.  From the Create (or Restructure) mode, move your cursor to the field in the Field Type column of the Struct table that corresponds to the field you want to key.

2.  Add an asterisk (*) at the end of the specified field type (for example, type **A10***).

# RESTRUCTURING A TABLE

You may find that the structure you originally defined when you created a table becomes inadequate for your needs. In that case, you can change the structure of a table, usually without disturbing the data within. Changes you can make include adding new fields, deleting existing fields, changing the order of fields, renaming fields, changing field types, changing field lengths, and adding or removing key fields. Whenever you change the size of a field type or delete a field, Paradox removes the field from all reports and forms on which it was previously placed.

• **NOTE**   Certain restructuring operations, such as reducing the size of a field type or removing a key field, may result in the removal of data from a table. In these instances, Paradox saves the removed data to one of two temporary tables called Keyviol and Problems. If either of these tables are created after you restructure your table, you should take immediate steps to avoid losing your data permanently.

**See Also**   *The Keyviol Table* and *The Problems Table* (this chapter).

Restructuring a table is sometimes necessary as a maintenance measure, particularly after you delete a large number of records. When you delete a record, Paradox does not free up the disk space that it formerly occupied; that space is still assigned to the deleted record. You recover this wasted space by restructuring the table.

## To Restructure a Table

1. Press F10 (Menu) from the Main mode and select Modify Restructure.

2. Enter the name of the desired table or press Enter and select from a menu of tables in the current directory. Paradox will place you in the Restructure mode and display the Struct table with the current structure of the table.

3. Make the desired changes to Struct.

4. Press F2 (Do-It!) when you are through.

## To Add a Field to an Existing Table

1. From the Restructure mode, move the cursor to the field name in the Struct table above which you want to add a field and press Ins. The field at the cursor's position will drop one row and leave a blank line for you to enter new data.

2. Enter the field name and field type for the new field.

3. Press F2 (Do-It!) to save the new structure.

## To Delete a Field from a Table

1. From the Restructure mode, move the cursor to the field name in the Struct table that you want to delete and press Del. Paradox will delete the field.

2. Press F2 (Do-It!) to save the new structure. Paradox will display the message Please confirm deletion of field along with the Delete and Oops! menu options.

3.  Select Delete to delete the field and restructure the table. Select Oops! to cancel the deletion and return to the Struct table.

You can delete any field in a table. If you delete a key field, however, one or more records may no longer be unique from other records for data in the key fields. Since data in key fields must be unique by definition, duplicated key-field records will be removed from a table when it is restructured and placed in the temporary table called Keyviol.

## To Change a Field Type

1.  From the Restructure mode, move to the desired field type entry in the Struct table and press Ctrl-Backspace to delete it.

2.  Enter a new field type.

3.  Press F2 (Do-It!). If the new field type is smaller or more restrictive than the old one, Paradox will display the message Possible data loss along with the Trimming, No-Trimming, and Oops! menu options.

4.  Select Trimming to truncate any field values that no longer fit in the field. Select No-Trimming to remove the records that contain field values that no longer fit in the field and place them in a temporary table called Problems. Select Oops! to return to the Struct table.

You can change a field from one type to another, as long as they are compatible. Table 2.2 lists the valid changes for each field type.

## To Move a Field in a Table

1.  From the Restructure mode, move the cursor to the new position in the Struct table for the field you are moving and press Ins.

2.  Enter the name of the field in the Field Type column and press Enter. (Spelling counts; capitalization does not.) Paradox will automatically move the field from its old position to this new location.

Paradox permits you to move a field easily from one location in a Struct table to another. This is usually only necessary when you want to add a key to a field that is neither the first field nor the first unkeyed field in a table.

**Table 2.2:** Permissible Field Type Changes

| ORIGINAL FIELD TYPE | PERMISSIBLE CHANGE(S) |
|---------------------|------------------------|
| Alphanumeric | Date |
| | Resize the alphanumeric field |
| Currency | Alphanumeric |
| | Numeric |
| | Short numeric |
| Date | Alphanumeric |
| Numeric | Alphanumeric |
| | Currency |
| | Short numeric |
| Short numeric | Alphanumeric |
| | Currency |
| | Numeric |

## To Add a Key to a Field

1.   From the Restructure mode, move the cursor to the field name in the Field Type column to which you want to add a key.

2.   Add an asterisk (*) after the field type. For example, type **A8*** to identify an A8 field type as a key field.

3.   Press F2 (Do-It!).

Any field in a table can be defined as a key field, but it must be located *above* any unkeyed fields in the Struct table. If it is not, you must first move it before adding the key.

● **NOTE**   The addition of a key field may result in key violations if the table was previously unkeyed. If duplicate values exist in the key field(s), Paradox will retain only one record for each unique key value in the table. Duplicate records will be placed in the temporary table called Keyviol.

## To Remove a Key from a Field

1.   From the Restructure mode, move to the key-field name in the Field Type column and use the Backspace key to erase the asterisk (*).

2.   Press F2 (Do-It!).

Paradox permits you to remove a key from one or all key fields in a table.

● **NOTE**   If a table has more than one key field, and you remove the key from some (but not all) of them, you may create a key violation. If some of the records contain the same values in the remaining key fields, only one record for each unique combination of key values will remain in the original table. Duplicate values will be placed in the temporary table called Keyviol.

# THE KEYVIOL TABLE

Any time a key violation occurs during table restructuring, Paradox keeps only one record for each unique key, and places the duplicate records in the Keyviol table. Paradox displays the Keyviol table and makes it current once restructuring is completed. If you do not want to lose the records placed in it, *you must take immediate action*. Rename the Keyviol table. This is important because Keyviol is a temporary table and, consequently, will be deleted if you exit

Paradox, change directories, or perform another operation that creates a Keyviol table.

You can return the key violation records back to the original table only if you change the tables so that key violations no longer exist. This involves either changing the structure of the original table or changing the data in one or both tables. Then you can add the Keyviol records back to the original table.

**See Also**    *Renaming Objects* (Chapter 8).

# THE PROBLEMS TABLE

When you change the field type of one or more fields during restructuring, Paradox removes any records from the table whose values cannot be accommodated by the new field type. These records are placed in the temporary table called Problems. If you do not want to lose these records, you should *immediately* rename Problems.

You can return the Problems records back to the original table only if you change the tables so that the field values can be accommodated. This involves either changing the structure of the original table or changing the data in the Problems table.

**See Also**    *Renaming Objects* (Chapter 8).

## Chapter Three

# VIEWING
# AND EDITING TABLES

This chapter describes how to view tables and enter and edit their data. Determining how data are displayed and improving the integrity of data are also covered. (By *integrity*, we mean the accuracy of your data, including maintaining the relationships between data stored in separate, yet related tables.)

# VIEWING TABLES

## To View a Table

1. Press F10 (Menu) from the Main mode and select View.

2. Enter the name of the table you want to view or press Enter to select from a menu of tables in the current directory.

**What For?** Viewing a table allows you to see your data. When you view a table, Paradox displays an image of it on the workspace, 22 records at a time.

• **DEFINITION** When the cursor is in a table or query image, that image is said to be *current*. If two or more images are on the workspace at any one time, only one of them can be current. Whenever you make an image current, Paradox places the cursor in the current record and field for that image.

## To Toggle between Table View and Form View

Press F7 (Form Toggle)

**What For?** When you first view a table, it is presented in a format called *table view*, where fields are represented as columns and records as rows. A table can also be viewed through a *form*. This format is called *form view*.

## To Move around a Table

Paradox provides a variety of keys that permit you to move the cursor around the current table in both table and form views. These keys are shown in Table 3.1.

**Table 3.1**: Keys for Moving around the Current Table

| Key | Effect |
|-----|--------|
| Backspace | Deletes character to the left of the cursor (only in Edit, CoEdit, or DataEntry) |
| Ctrl–Backspace | Deletes entire entry in field (only in Edit, CoEdit, or DataEntry) |
| Ctrl–End | Moves cursor to the last field of the current record |
| Ctrl–Home | Moves cursor to the first field of the current record |
| Ctrl–← | Moves one screenful of fields to the left in table view |
| Ctrl–PgDn | Moves cursor to the same field in the next record (only in form view) |
| Ctrl–PgUp | Moves cursor to the same field in the previous record (only in form view) |
| Ctrl–→ | Moves one screenful of fields to the right in table view |
| Del | Deletes entire record (only in Edit, CoEdit, or Data Entry) |
| End | Moves cursor to the last record |
| Enter | Moves cursor to the next field |
| Esc | Displays message Escape only active when menu is displayed—Press [F10] to display menu |
| Home | Moves cursor to the first record |
| Ins | Inserts a new record above where the cursor is currently located (only in Edit, CoEdit, or Data Entry) |
| ← | Moves cursor to the left one field |
| → | Moves cursor to the right one field |
| PgDn | Displays next screenful of records (in table view) or page of a form (in form view) |

**Table 3.1:** Keys for Moving around the Current Table (continued)

| Key | Effect |
|-----|--------|
| PgUp | Displays previous screenful of records (in table view) or page of a form (in form view) |
| ↑ | Moves cursor up one record (only in table view) |
| ↓ | Moves cursor down one record (only in table view) |
| F3 (Up Image) | On a multi-table form, moves to the previous table (master table or detail table) within a multi-table form |
| F4 | (Down Image) On a multi-table form, moves to the next table (master table or detail table) within a multi-table form |

## To Use Field View

1. From any mode, move to the field in which you want to enter field view.

2. Press Ctrl–F (Field View) or Alt–F5 (Field View). Paradox places you in field view and changes the cursor-position indicator to a block character.

3. To exit field view, press Enter.

**What For?** Field view allows you to move within a field. This is useful when you want to edit part of a field or display a field that is too big for the column size (table view) or field width (form view). The keys for editing the contents of a field in this viewing mode are shown in Table 3.2.

● **NOTE** Field view can also be used to edit any field in Paradox where a typed response is required, such as the prompt that asks you to provide a table name.

**Table 3.2**: Keys for Moving around the Current Field

| Key | Effect |
| --- | --- |
| Backspace | Deletes character to the left of the cursor |
| Ctrl–Backspace | Deletes entire entry |
| Ctrl– ← | Moves cursor one word to the left |
| Ctrl– → | Moves cursor one word to the right |
| Del | Deletes character at the cursor |
| ↓ | Moves cursor down one line in a word-wrapped field |
| End | Moves cursor to the last character |
| Enter | Exits field view |
| Esc | Displays menu or a message instructing you to press F10 (Menu) |
| Home | Moves cursor to the first character |
| Ins | Toggles between insert and writeover modes |
| ← | Moves cursor to the left one character |
| → | Moves cursor to the right one character |
| ↑ | Moves cursor up one line in a word-wrapped field |

# EDITING A TABLE

There are two modes that permit you to add, delete, and change data in a table: Edit and CoEdit. While you are in either of these modes, you will not be able to add or remove tables from the workspace. Therefore, it is necessary first to display (view) all of the tables you want to edit at one time on the workspace before entering Edit or CoEdit.

# To Enter Edit or CoEdit Mode

1. Press F10 (Menu) from the Main mode and select Modify Edit or Modify CoEdit.

2. Enter the name of the table you want to edit or press Enter and select from a menu of tables in the current directory.

3. Press F2 (Do-It!) when you are done editing the table.

You can also enter the Edit or CoEdit modes when one or more tables are already on the workspace:

1. View the table(s) on the workspace.

2. Press F9 (Edit) or Alt–F9 (CoEdit).

3. Edit the table(s) and press F3 (Up Image) and F4 (Down Image) to move between them on the workspace.

4. Press F2 (Do-It!) when you are done editing.

**What For?** Edit and CoEdit differ in how they update a table. In Edit mode, new records that contain the same key values as existing records will automatically replace them without warning, once you press F2 (Do-It!). In CoEdit mode, by contrast, you will be warned as soon as you move the cursor off a record that duplicates existing key values—at which point you can press Alt–L to replace the existing record or Alt–K to display the values from the existing record.

In Edit mode, Paradox only updates the order of records based on the key fields when you end the Edit session. With CoEdit, the record order is updated each time the cursor leaves a record.

You can undo the last change made to a table in either Edit or CoEdit mode. In CoEdit, only the *last* change can be undone, while in Edit you can undo *all* changes made during an editing session by using Undo repeatedly.

Finally, no other users may access a table that you are editing in Edit mode. In CoEdit mode, however, other users may view, report, query, and even edit the same table you are editing. The only restriction with CoEdit is that two users cannot edit the same record at the same time.

The Edit menu is displayed any time you press F10 (Menu) while you are in the Edit mode. The Edit menu options are as follows:

**Image:** Accesses the Image menu to allow you to modify the way a table is displayed

**Undo:** Undoes the last change to a record. Undo can be used repeatedly to undo successive, previous changes to a table

**ValCheck:** Places restrictions on valid entries for fields

**Help:** Accesses the help system

**DO-IT!:** Saves changes made to a table during the current editing session

**Cancel:** Cancels all changes made to a table during the current editing session

The CoEdit menu is displayed any time you press F10 (Menu) while you are in the CoEdit mode:

**Image:** Accesses the Image menu to allow you to modify the way a table is displayed

**Undo:** Undoes the last change to a record

**AutoRefresh:** Changes the length of the automatic refresh period, the time between which the contents of a table are updated to reflect the changes that other users have made to it

**Help:** Accesses the help system

**DO-IT!:** Saves changes made to a table during the current editing session

## To Undo a Change

1.  Press Ctrl–U or select Undo from either the Edit, CoEdit, or DataEntry menu.

2.  If you are in Edit or DataEntry mode, you can continue undoing each previously made change by repeating Step 1.

# SORTING RECORDS IN A TABLE

## To Sort a Table

1. Press F10 (Menu) from the Main mode and select Modify Sort.

2. Enter the name of the desired table or press Enter and select from a menu of tables in the current directory.

3. If the table is keyed, enter a name for a new sorted table that Paradox should create. If the table is not keyed, select whether Paradox should sort the records to the same table or create a new table to hold the sorted records. If you select New, enter the name of the new table to be created.

4. Move the cursor to the field that will determine the first sorting of records and type **1**.

5. If you want to sort on two or more fields, move the cursor to the second field and type **2**, and so on.

6. To sort a field in a descending order (rather than the default ascending order), move to the field and enter **D** after the sort-order number.

7. Press F2 (Do-It!).

# USING DATAENTRY

## To Use DataEntry

1. Press F10 (Menu) from the Main mode and select Modify DataEntry.

**2.** Enter the name of the table for which you want to create an Entry table or press Enter and select from a menu of tables in the current directory. Paradox will place you in the DataEntry mode.

**3.** Enter data in the displayed Entry table.

**4.** To add these records to the existing table, press F2 (Do-It!).

**What For?**  Paradox's DataEntry feature allows you to add records to a temporary table, called Entry, that has the same structure as an existing table. You can then insert all of the new records at one time to the existing table. This feature is particularly useful when your tables are stored in a shared directory on a network.

## To Save Records in the Entry Table

Press F10 (Menu) from the DataEntry mode and select KeepEntry.

**What For?**  Once you have entered data in the Entry table, you have the option of *not* adding the records immediately to the existing table, but saving them to the Entry table itself. One situation in which you may want to do this is when the existing table is currently locked by another user. After saving the Entry table, you should immediately rename it with the Rename tool, since Paradox will delete any table named Entry when you either change directories, begin another DataEntry session, or end your Paradox session.

**See Also**  *Renaming Objects* (Chapter 8).

# USING MULTIENTRY

## To Use MultiEntry

**1.** Press F10 (Menu) from the Main mode and select Modify MultiEntry Entry.

2. Enter the name of the source table whose structure will define the Entry table, or press Enter and select from a menu of tables in the current directory.

3. Enter the name of the MultiEntry map table or press Enter and select from a menu of tables in the current directory. Paradox places you in the DataEntry mode.

4. Enter data in the displayed Entry table.

5. Press F2 (Do-It!) to insert the data into the appropriate tables.

**What For?** Paradox's MultiEntry feature allows you to add records to a temporary table, called Entry, that has the same structure as an existing table. You can then insert all of the new records at one time to two or more related tables.

• **NOTE** Before you can use MultiEntry for the first time, you must set up the MultiEntry feature. You can also save the contents of the Entry table after a MultiEntry session by renaming it.

## To Set Up MultiEntry

1. From the Main mode, construct a query on the workspace. Use examples to link related fields in the two or more tables displayed on the workspace. Use check marks to in-clude fields in the source table.

2. Press F10 (Menu) and select Modify MultiEntry Setup.

3. Enter the name for the source table that will hold the struc-ture to be used in the Entry table during MultiEntry.

4. Enter the name of the table that will hold the MultiEntry map.

**What For?** Before you use Paradox's MultiEntry feature for the first time, you must perform a MultiEntry setup. This involves creat-ing a query on the workspace (described in Chapter 6) that defines the relationship between your two or more tables. In it, you use *examples* to link the related tables on the basis of one or more fields and *check marks* to include fields from the query in the MultiEntry table. Once you define this query, the MultiEntry setup procedure creates two tables. The *source table* contains the structure to be used in the Entry table when you enter data. The *map table* defines how data in the fields of the Entry table are to be placed into your two or more related tables.

**See Also** *Making Queries* and *Queries of Two or More Tables* (Chapter 6); *Renaming Objects* (Chapter 8).

# THE IMAGE MENU

The Image menu contains six, seven, or eight menu options, depending on which mode you are in. (Graph is not displayed when you are in the Edit, CoEdit, or DataEntry mode; KeepSet is not displayed in the DataEntry mode.) Following are the Image menu options:

**TableSize:** Specifies the number of records in a table to display at one time

**ColumnSize:** Changes the displayed width of a field

**Format:** Modifies the format for displaying numeric, currency, and date fields

**Zoom:** Moves the cursor to a specified field, record, or value in a field

**Move:** Changes the display order of fields in a table

**PickForm:** Selects the preferred (default) form for a table

**KeepSet:** Saves the image settings for later use

**Graph:** Creates a Crosstab table or a graph (covered in Chapter 7)

## To Display the Image Menu

1. From either the Main, Edit, CoEdit, or DataEntry mode, make current the table to which you want to apply image settings.

2. Press F10 (Menu) and select Image.

## To Adjust the Table Size

1. From either the Main, Edit, CoEdit, or DataEntry mode, press F10 (Menu) and select Image TableSize.

2. Press ↑ and ↓ until the table displays the desired number of records and press Enter.

**What For?** To display up to 22 records of a table at one time in table view (22 is the maximum when no other images are present; they take up the entire workspace). You can adjust the size of the table so that fewer records are displayed at one time.

## To Adjust the Column Size

1. From either the Main, Edit, CoEdit, or DataEntry mode, press F10 (Menu) and select Image ColumnSize.

2. Move the cursor to the column you want to size and press Enter.

3. Use ← and → to define the new width of the selected column and press Enter.

**What For?** To define a column width to be *less* than the width selected by Paradox. (Paradox automatically defines the width of fields in a table or query image in table view.) You cannot, however, adjust the column width to be *wider* than the Paradox default, the maximum field width, or 78 columns, whichever is greater.

## To Change the Display Format of a Field

1. From the Main, Edit, CoEdit, or DataEntry mode, press F10 (Menu) and select Image Format.

2. Move the cursor to the field you want to format and press Enter.

3. If the field is a date field, select the desired Date format. Otherwise, select one of the following types of formats: General, Fixed, Comma, or Scientific.

**4.** Define the format (as described in the following sections) and press Enter.

**What For?** Based on the field type, Paradox selects a default format for displaying numeric, currency, and date fields. This procedure allows you to change the format of data in these fields. (The display formats for alphanumeric and short numeric fields cannot be changed.)

The various formats are described as follows:

- The **General** format option for a numeric or currency field lets you define the maximum number of decimal places to display. For example, if you set it to 3, and do not define a fixed format, the number 5 will be displayed as 5, the number 5.25 will be displayed as 5.25, and 5.12345 will be displayed as 5.123.

- The **Fixed** format option permits you to specify how many decimal places to display, regardless of the value stored in the field. For example, if you define a fixed format of 3, the number 5 will be displayed as 5.000 and 5.12345 will be displayed as 5.123.

- The **Comma** option allows you to display data with commas, since you cannot use commas directly when you enter data in a numeric or currency field. When you select it, you must also specify the number of decimal places to which you want to display the values.

- The **Scientific** option allows you to display all numbers in scientific notation, regardless of their size. Generally, if you enter a very large number in a numeric or currency field, Paradox will automatically display the number in scientific notation by default. And if you enter smaller numbers in scientific notation, Paradox will automatically convert them to decimal notation by default. When you select the Scientific option, you must also specify the number of decimal places.

- Paradox supports three **Date** formats for date field entries: MM/DD/YY, DD–Mon–YY, and DD.MM.YY. Although you can enter data in a date field using any of these three formats, they will be displayed in only the format you choose.

# To Zoom to a Field, Record, or Value

1. From the Main, Edit, CoEdit, or DataEntry mode, press F10 (Menu) and select Image Zoom.

2. Select whether you want to zoom to a field, record, or value.

3. Indicate the desired field, record, or value as follows:

   • If you selected Field, choose the desired field from the menu displayed.

   • If you selected Record, enter the desired record number.

   • If you selected Value, move to the field containing the data you want to search through and press Enter. Next, enter the exact value you want to search for (capitalization matters), or use wildcards in conjunction with a string to match. Press Enter when done.

**What For?**   The Zoom option allows you to move the cursor instantly to a given field, record number, or value within a field. This feature is particularly useful for moving around in large tables.

# To Use a Wildcard in a Zoom

Include an @ character or two dots (..) in your string to search for when you zoom to a value.

Below are some examples of the wildcard characters in strings:

| | | |
|---|---|---|
| @and | *would zoom to* | Band, land, HAND |
| ..and | *would zoom to* | AND, stand, overland |
| @and.. | *would zoom to* | sands, dandy, landing |
| ..a@t.. | *would zoom to* | ant, tantrum, asterisk |

**What For?**   You can use wildcard characters to zoom to values based on patterns in the values instead of exact matches. The @ represents one character of any value; the two dots represent zero, one, or more characters of any value. When you use wildcards to search for a pattern, capitalization is ignored.

## To Search for a Value or Pattern

1. From the Main, Edit, CoEdit, or DataEntry mode, place the cursor in the field in which you want to zoom and press Ctrl–Z (Zoom).

2. Enter a value or pattern and press Enter. If Paradox finds a match to your value or pattern in the current field, it will move the cursor to the first record that contains the match. If no match is found, the message Match not found will be displayed.

3. If Paradox has found a match, you can move to the next one by pressing Alt–Z (Zoom Next). Doing so repeatedly allows you to scan a table quickly for all matches to your chosen value or pattern.

## To Move a Field in a Table

1. From the Main, Edit, CoEdit, or DataEntry mode, press F10 (Menu) and select Image Move.

2. Select the field you want to move from the displayed menu of fields for the current table.

3. Move the cursor to the position where you want to move the field and press Enter.

**What For?**    To display a table's fields in any order, regardless of its structure.

Instead of selecting Move from the Image menu, you can use Ctrl–R (Rotate) to rearrange the display order of fields in a table. When the cursor is current on a table, pressing Ctrl–R (Rotate) moves the current field to the last (rightmost) field position in the table. All of the fields to the right of the current field are shifted to the left by one field position.

## To Pick a Preferred Form

1. From the Main, Edit, CoEdit, or DataEntry mode, make the desired table the current image on the workspace and press F10 (Menu).

2. Select Image PickForm to have Paradox display the available forms for the current table.

3. Select a form. If you have not designed any forms for the table, only the standard form (F) will be available.

**What For?**  Use the PickForm option to display a table in a particular form. Once you select a form, press F7 (Form Toggle) to toggle between your *preferred form* and table view.

## To Keep the Settings for a Table Image

1. From the Main, Edit, or CoEdit mode, define one or more image settings for a table.

2. Press F10 (Menu) and select Image KeepSet.

**What For?**  As soon as you clear an image from the workspace, its image settings are lost. The KeepSet option, therefore, allows you to save the current image settings for a table (with the exception of the TableSize setting). The table will then use these settings whenever it is on the workspace.

● **NOTE**  To change the table settings after you have used KeepSet, redefine the settings and then use KeepSet again. Remove any of these settings with the Delete tool.

# USING VALCHECKS

ValChecks are definitions that specify acceptable values for a field. Although they are optional, judicious use of ValChecks can simplify data entry and reduce the likelihood of errors. There are six different ValChecks: LowValue, HighValue, Default, Table-Lookup, Picture, and Required.

## To Apply a ValCheck to a Field

1.  From the Edit or DataEntry mode, press F10 (Menu) and select ValCheck Define.

2.  Move the cursor to the field for which you want to define a ValCheck and press Enter.

3.  Select the type of ValCheck you want to apply (see below).

4.  If you select Required, you are done. To define any other type of ValCheck, enter the appropriate definition and press Enter.

**What For?**   During data entry, values entered in a table are compared with the ValChecks. If Paradox detects a value that is incompatible with a ValCheck, the value will not be accepted in the field and an error message will be displayed. ValChecks do not affect data already entered in a table, data entered as a result of an insert query, or data added from one table to another. Also, the table containing the field to which you want to define a ValCheck must be the current table.

Below are the types of ValCheck options from which to choose:

*   The **LowValue** and **HighValue** ValChecks are used to define the lowest and highest values that can be entered into a field

*   When you define a **Default** ValCheck, Paradox will automatically enter this exact entry in a field if you leave it empty. Date fields can be defined with a special default entry. When you enter **today** as the Default ValCheck, the current date will appear in a field if you leave it blank. This date is based on your computer's internal clock

*   **Picture** can be used to automate data entry in a field as well as force formatting characteristics onto entries in a field. Table 3.3 contains the available picture characters and their uses. Table 3.4 displays examples of pictures and their effects

**Table 3.3**: Picture Characters

| Picture Specifier | Effect |
|---|---|
| # | Specifies one number only |
| ? | Specifies one letter only |
| & | Specifies one letter only, converted to upper case |
| @ | Specifies one character of any type |
| ! | Specifies one character of any type, with all letters being converted to upper case |
| * | Repeats of next specification |
| [ ] | Identifies optional specifier |
| { } | Groups alternatives |
| , | Separates alternatives |
| ; | Takes the next character literally (for use with any of the above picture specifiers) |

**Table 3.4**: Examples of Pictures

| Picture | Example of Usage |
|---|---|
| ###-##-#### | Social Security numbers |
| [(###)]###-####[*#] | U.S. phone numbers. The optional numbers at the end of the specification are for extensions |
| &*? | Capitalizes the first letter of a word of any length |
| $*#.## | Dollar values |

**Table 3.4:** Examples of Pictures (continued)

| Picture | Example of Usage |
|---|---|
| YES,NO | Accepts only the entry **YES** or **NO** |
| B{l{ue,ack},rown} | Accepts only the values **Blue, Black**, or **Brown** |
| *# ; @ $*#.## | Accepts an entry specifying a number at a dollar amount (for example **7 @ $12.56** or **100 @ $125.75**) |
| *[{&,[*#]}{ ,–,*?}*[&*?[[@][ ][ ]]]] | Accepts addresses, capitalizing the first letter of each word |

- A **Required** ValCheck guarantees that a value is entered in a field. However, this is not enforced unless the cursor lands in the required field while in Edit, CoEdit, or Data Entry mode

- A **TableLookup** ValCheck is useful when all the acceptable values for a field appear in the first field of a second table, for instance, when a part-number field in an invoice table only contains values that appear in the first key-field in a part table. By applying a TableLookup ValCheck, only those values appearing in the first field of the second table will be allowed in the field with the TableLookup ValCheck. Following are the additional steps you perform once you select TableLookup:

  1. Enter the name of the table containing the lookup values or press Enter and select from a menu of tables in the current directory.
  2. Select JustCurrentField or AllCorrespondingFields.
  3. Select PrivateLookup or HelpAndFill.

If you select JustCurrentField, Paradox will influence only the field to which the TableLookup ValCheck was applied. If you select AllCorrespondingFields, Paradox will automatically copy data from all lookup-table fields that share the exact same field names to the corresponding fields in the table you are editing.

If you select PrivateLookup, Paradox will simply compare the value you entered in a field with the Lookup table entries. If you select HelpAndFill, a prompt will appear whenever a table is in Edit or CoEdit mode and the cursor is in a field with a TableLookup ValCheck. This prompt reads Press F1 for help with fill-in. When you press F1, Paradox will display the Lookup table. You can then move the cursor to the record that contains the desired value and press F2 (Do-It!) to have Paradox automatically enter the lookup value into the field you are editing.

## To Remove ValChecks from the Current Table

1. From the Edit or DataEntry mode, press F10 (Menu) and select ValCheck Clear.

2. Select Field to remove ValChecks from a single field or All to remove ValChecks from all fields in the current table.

3. If you selected Field, move the cursor to the field from which you want to remove the ValChecks and press Enter.

● **NOTE**   You may also delete a ValCheck definition from an entire table with the Delete tool. You cannot remove just *one* of the multiple ValChecks defined for a field; however, you can redefine it.

**See Also**   *Copying and Deleting Objects* (Chapter 8).

## Chapter Four

# DESIGNING FORMS

This chapter describes how to design and change forms. A form is like a window through which you view, enter, and edit data contained in a table. It can be designed to include either all fields from a table or only those fields you want to edit. Most forms are used to display data in a table, one record at a time. But it is also possible to display more than one record at once, as well as data from two or more tables simultaneously.

In addition to displaying fields from tables, forms can include text, boxes and borders, and general organizational features that make entering and working with data easier. A representative form is shown in Figure 4.1.

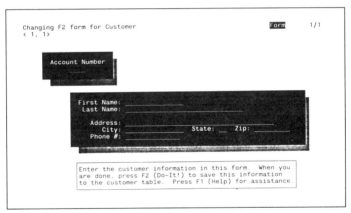

**Figure 4.1:** Customized form

# DESIGNING AND CHANGING FORMS

When you custom-design a form for a table, you assign it a number from 1 to 14. If you do not custom-design a form, Paradox will automatically use the standard form, F, when you display the table in form view. Each table can have up to 15 forms associated with it (F plus 1–14).

You can always change a form you have previously designed. The steps involved in designing or changing a form are similar, and require you to specify both a table name and form number. Paradox then displays the form-design screen, where you design and change forms.

## To Design a Form

1. Press F10 (Menu) from the Main mode and select Forms Design.

2. Enter the name of the table for which the form is being designed, or press Enter to select from a menu of tables in the current directory.

3. Select a form (F or 1–14).

4. Enter an informative description for this form and press Enter. Paradox will display the form-design screen shown in Figure 4.2.

## To Change an Existing Form

1. Press F10 (Menu) from the Main mode and select Forms Change.

2. Enter the name of the table to which the form belongs. Alternatively, press Enter and select from a menu of tables in the current directory.

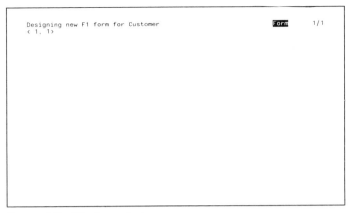

```
Designing new F1 form for Customer                    Form       1/1
< 1, 1>
```

**Figure 4.2:** The form-design screen

  **3.**  Select the existing form you want to change from the dis-
       played menu of forms.

  **4.**  Modify the form description, if desired, and press Enter.
       Paradox will display the form-design screen shown in
       Figure 4.2.

The message at the top left of the form-design screen specifies the
form you are designing or changing. At the top right of the menu
is the mode indicator showing that you are in Form mode, as well
as the insert toggle-indicator and page number (current page out of
total number of pages). The second line of the menu lists the
<row,column> cursor position, the type of field in which the cursor
is currently located, and the name of that field. The rest of the
screen is where you design or change the form.

**See Also**    Chapter 3 for information on how to enter data with
a form.

## To Move around the Form-Design Screen

  Use the keys shown in Table 4.1.

**Table 4.1**: Keys Used in the Form-Design Screen

| Key | Effect |
|---|---|
| Ctrl–End | Moves cursor to the rightmost column |
| Ctrl–Home | Moves cursor to the leftmost column |
| Del | Deletes character at the cursor |
| ↓ | Moves down one line |
| End | Moves to the last line on a form |
| Enter | Moves down one line |
| Home | Moves to the first line on a form |
| Ins | Toggles between Insert and Typeover modes |
| ← | Moves cursor to the left |
| Page Down | Displays next page of a multi-page form |
| Page Up | Displays previous page of a multi-page form |
| → | Moves cursor to the right |
| ↑ | Moves up one line |

# THE FORM MENU

The Form menu provides access to Paradox's form-designing features. The menu options are as follows:

**Field:** Places, modifies, or removes fields

**Area:** Moves or erases blocks of fields and/or text

**Border:** Places or erases borders

**Page:** Adds additional pages to create a multi-page form, or deletes existing pages

**Style:** Applies color, highlighting, and other attributes

**Multi:** Creates and modifies multi-table and multi-record forms

**Help:** Displays help information

**DO-IT!:** Saves the form and returns to the Main menu

**Cancel:** Cancels all changes made to a form since the last save and returns to the Main menu

# PLACING A FIELD IN A FORM

You can include all or only a subset of the fields from a table on a form. At a minimum, Paradox requires that at least one regular field be placed on a form in order to save it. When a field is placed on a form, its position is indicated with a series of dashes. These dashes only appear while you are designing or changing a form. When you view data in form view, the data from a field in a table appear at the location on the form where the field is placed.

## To Place a Field in a Form

1.  Press F10 (Menu) from the Form mode and select Field Place.

2.  Select Regular, DisplayOnly, Calculated, or #Record.

3.  If you select Regular or DisplayOnly, choose the desired field from the displayed menu of fields. If you select Calculated, enter a valid calculation and press Enter. If you select #Record, continue to the next step.

4.  Move the cursor on the form to where you want the field's leftmost position to begin and press Enter.

5.  Adjust the size of the field with the ←, →, and Home keys and press Enter.

## TYPES OF FIELDS

There are four types of fields:

- **Regular fields** are the ones in which you enter or edit data. Each field from a table may appear on a given form only once as a regular field, so the menu of regular fields that Paradox displays will not include those fields that have already been placed on the form

- **DisplayOnly fields** are similar to regular fields. As their name suggests, they display only the field values. You cannot enter or edit the contents of these fields or use zoom on them

- **#Record fields** display the record number for the current record on a form. Note that if you display a #Record field on a linked, embedded form, the record number displayed will be the position of the record in the restricted view of the embedded form's *detail table* (see *Multi-table Forms*, this chapter)

- **Calculated fields** display information not actually stored in a table; they combine data from regular fields, certain PAL functions, constants, and variables to form *new* fields. As with DisplayOnly fields, you cannot enter or edit the contents of calculated fields or zoom on them. The formula you enter in a calculation is called an *expression*

  There are three different types of calculated fields: alphanumeric, numeric, and date. Alphanumeric expressions accept only the + operator for concatenating alphanumeric fields, constants, or functions. Numeric operators use +, −, *, and / for addition, subtraction, multiplication, and division, respectively. Date expressions accept only + and − for performing date arithmetic.

  To use a regular-field value in an expression, you must enclose the field name in square brackets. For example, a field called First Name would be specified as **[First Name]**. Although alphanumeric constants in an expression are enclosed in double quotes, numeric and date constants are not. Any variable defined by a PAL script (including a MiniScript) can be included in an expression, or even as the argument for a PAL function. It is not necessary for a variable to be defined when a calculated field is placed on a form, but it must be defined when the form is used. Functions can be used in expressions if the value that the function returns is compatible with the remaining elements of the expression.

An expression can be up to 175 characters long. Examples of valid expressions in calculated fields are shown in Table 4.2.

**Table 4.2:** Examples of Expressions

| Expression | Expression Type |
|---|---|
| [First Name]+" "+[Last Name] | Alphanumeric |
| FORMAT("W20,AC",[Comment]) | Alphanumeric |
| "Date due: "+STRVAL([Due Date]) | Alphanumeric |
| [Total price]*.07 | Numeric |
| [Invoice Date]+30 | Date |

**See Also** *PAL Functions in Forms and Reports* (Appendix A).

# CHANGING A PLACED FIELD

There are a number of changes you can make to a field once it is placed. These include erasing a field, changing the field width, editing a calculated field, or making the contents of long fields wrap over two or more lines.

## To Erase a Field

1. Press F10 (Menu) from the Form mode and select Field Erase.

2. Move the cursor to the field you want to erase and press Enter.

**What For?**   To erase a field from a form either when you no longer need to display the field or when you want to change its position. To change a field's position, first erase the field and then replace it at the new position.

## To Reformat a Field's Width

1. Press F10 (Menu) from the Form mode and select Field Reformat.

2. Move the cursor to the field on the form you want to reformat and press Enter.

3. Use the ←, →, and Home keys to define the new width of the field and press Enter.

**What For?**   To change the width of an existing field on a form. This width cannot be wider than the width originally defined for the field's type, however.

## To Edit a Calculated Field

1. Press F10 (Menu) from the Form mode and select Field CalcEdit.

2. Move the cursor to the calculated field you want to edit and press Enter.

3. Make changes to the displayed calculation. Ctrl–F or Alt–F5 (Field View) allow you to edit the calculation in field view. Press Enter when you are finished.

**What For?**   To edit a calculated expression *without* having to erase and then replace a calculated field.

## To Wordwrap a Field

1. Press F10 (Menu) from the Form mode and select Field WordWrap.

2. Move the cursor to the desired field and press Enter.

3. Type a number indicating the total number of lines (including the first line) on which text in a field can be displayed. Then press Enter.

**What For?** Since some alphanumeric fields, by definition, are too long to fit on a single line (fields with field types greater than the screen width, A80, for instance), you can display the contents of fields on more than one line. This technique is called *wordwrapping* and can be used with an alphanumeric field of any size.

To use wordwrap, you define the width of a field so that it equals the length of the first line of the wordwrapped area. You then specify the total number of lines for wordwrapping text in a field. When the form is displayed, any text that does not fit on the first line of the field will be wrapped over to the line(s) beneath.

● **NOTE** While you are designing or changing a form, you will not see the additional lines of a wordwrapped field. Instead, when you move the cursor onto a wordwrapped field, the indicator wrap:n (where *n* is the number of lines that the field wraps onto) will be displayed in the right menu-area next to the field name. Even though you cannot see the additional wordwrapped lines, Paradox will not permit you to place other fields or text in the space allotted to them.

# AREA OPERATIONS

While designing or changing a form, you define a rectangular region of the form as an *area*. This area, including all of the fields and text contained in it, can then be moved to another location on the form or erased. Each of these operations is described next.

## To Move an Area

**1.** Press F10 (Menu) from the Form mode and select Area Move.

**2.** Move the cursor to one of the corners of a rectangle that defines the area you want to move and press Enter.

**3.** Move the cursor to the opposite corner of the rectangle and press Enter. Paradox highlights the defined area as shown in Figure 4.3.

**4.** Use the arrow keys to move the defined area to a new position and press Enter.

**What For?** Moving an area provides a convenient way to adjust the way a form appears. All fields you want to move must be entirely within the area you define.

## To Erase an Area

**1.** Press F10 (Menu) from the Form mode and select Area Erase.

**2.** Move the cursor to one of the corners of a rectangle that defines the area you want to erase and press Enter.

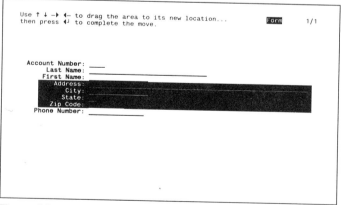

**Figure 4.3:** Defining an area on a form

3. Move the cursor to the opposite corner of the rectangle and press Enter.

## To Place a Border

1. Press F10 (Menu) from the Form mode and select Border Place.

2. Select a Single, Double, or Other border style.

3. If you select Other, enter the single character you want to use for the border.

4. Move the cursor to one corner of a rectangle where you want to place the border and press Enter.

5. Move the cursor to the opposite corner of the rectangle and press Enter.

**What For?** Borders are useful for visually separating distinct areas of a form into sections. They greatly enhance the effectiveness as well as attractiveness of a form. Examples of Single and Double border styles are shown in Figure 4.4. The border consisting of X's was created with the Other border style.

```
Changing F1 form for Customer                        Form      1/1
< 1, 1>
XXXXXXXXXXXXXXXXXXXXXXXXXXXXXXXXXXXXXXXXXXXXXXXXXXXXXXXXXXXXXXXXXXX
X                                                                X
X                                        Account Number: ____    X
X                                        Record Number: ____     X
X                                                                X
X                                                                X
X                                                                X
X         First Name: _____                             X
X          Last Name: _____                         X
X                                                                X
X                                                                X
X     Address: _____          X
X        City: _____                                    X
X       State: __                                               X
X    Zip Code: _____                                        X
X                                                                X
X                                                                X
X             Phone Number: _____                     X
X                                                                X
X                                                                X
XXXXXXXXXXXXXXXXXXXXXXXXXXXXXXXXXXXXXXXXXXXXXXXXXXXXXXXXXXXXXXXXXX
```

**Figure 4.4:** Examples of border styles

## To Erase a Border

1.  Press F10 (Menu) from the Form mode and select Border Erase.

2.  Move the cursor to a corner of the border you want to erase and press Enter.

3.  Move the cursor to the opposite corner to define all or part of the border you want to erase and press Enter. Paradox will erase the defined part of the border.

# MULTI-PAGE FORMS

## To Create a Multi-page Form

1.  Press F10 (Menu) from the Form mode and select Page Insert.

2.  Select whether the inserted page should be placed before or after the current page.

3.  Place at least one regular field on the new page of the form before you attempt to save the form.

**What For?**   To create forms up to 15 pages in length. The one restriction for multi-page forms is that each page must contain at least one regular field.

## To Remove Unwanted Pages from a Multi-page Form

1.  Use the Page Up and Page Down keys to move the cursor to the page you want to delete.

2.  Press F10 (Menu) from the Form mode and select Page Delete. Paradox will ask you to confirm your request.

3.  Select Ok.

# DEFINING STYLE FEATURES

Paradox has a number of stylistic tools that allow you to modify the look of a form, enhancing its usefulness and attractiveness. These features include adding color, highlighting fields or text, and specifying that fields or text blink. You can also display the names of fields to aid you while you are designing or changing a form.

## To Add Color

1.  Press F10 (Menu) from the Form mode and select Style Color.

2.  Select Area to add color to an area or Border to add a colored, rectangular frame.

3.  Move the cursor to one corner of the area or border you want to color and press Enter.

4.  Move the cursor to the opposite corner and press Enter. Paradox will display the color palette.

5.  Move the cursor to the row and column position on the color palette that defines, respectively, the background (row) and foreground (column) colors you want. Press Enter to select that color combination.

**What For?**   To specify the colors that Paradox uses for areas or borders on your form. When you select a color, you choose both a foreground color, used for text, and a background color.

• **NOTE**   After Step 4 above, you can toggle the display of the color palette off and on by pressing Alt–C. When it is off, you'll see the names of the colors in the upper-right corner of the screen instead. You can still use the cursor keys as in Step 5 to change the color combination.

# To Apply Monochrome Attributes to a Form

1.   Press F10 (Menu) from the Form mode and select Style Monochrome.

2.   Select Area or Border to apply attributes, respectively, to an area or rectangular border surrounding an area.

3.   Move the cursor to one corner of the area or border to which you want to apply attributes and press Enter.

4.   Move the cursor to the opposite corner and press Enter. Paradox will display the current monochrome attribute at the upper right of the screen.

5.   Press ← and → until the desired attribute combination is displayed and press Enter.

**What For?**   To apply monochrome attributes such as reverse video or blinking to areas or borders on a form.

# To Show or Hide Field Names

1.   Press F10 (Menu) from the Form mode and select Style Fieldnames.

2.   Select Show to display the field names, or Hide to suppress their display.

**What For?**   You can display the actual name of a field at its location on a form to assist you while you are designing or changing a form. (Otherwise, only dashes indicate a field's position on a form.) If a field name is longer than the field format, only part of the name will be shown.

# To Control Highlighting in Multi-record Forms

1.   Press F10 (Menu) from the Form mode and select Style ShowHighlight.

2.   Select Hide to turn off the highlighting of multi-record regions on a form. To restore the highlighting, select Show.

**What For?** Since multi-record regions on a multi-record form are highlighted by default, you may wish to turn off this highlighting.

**See Also** *Multi-record Forms* (this chapter).

# MULTI-TABLE FORMS

A multi-table form allows you to display fields from one table, called the *master table*, with fields from other tables. You create a multi-table form by embedding forms designed for other tables (called *detail tables*) on it so that their fields are also displayed. These forms are called *embedded forms*.

A multi-table form can contain up to nine embedded forms, each of which can be either linked or unlinked to records in the master table, and can be either single- or multi-record forms.

## To Create a Multi-table Form

1. Design a form for each detail table that you will later embed on the multi-table form. The design of the form may vary depending on whether it is linked or unlinked.

2. Create a form for the master table.

3. Place the embedded form(s) on the master-table form to make it a multi-table form.

These are the general steps for creating a multi-table form. Refer to the following sections for more detailed descriptions of specific steps.

● **NOTE** When you view two or more tables through a multi-table form, Paradox places a *form lock* on them. This means that if you are working on a local area network (LAN), no other users will be allowed to access any of the involved tables unless they also use the same multi-table form.

## LINKED VS. UNLINKED FORMS

Linked embedded forms are applicable only when there is a one-to-one or a one-to-many relationship between the master table and detail table(s). In all cases, the detail table(s) must be keyed (the master need not necessarily be). The combination of one or more detail-table key fields must correspond to one or more fields in the master table. It is these related fields that makes the link possible.

When you view a multi-table form containing a linked embedded form, the embedded form displays only those records from the detail table that are related to the record displayed on the master table. This limited view of the detail table's records is called the *restricted view*. If there is a one-to-one relationship between the master table and the detail table, only one record from the detail table can match the master table record. If there is a one-to-many relationship, one or more records may match. In these cases, the embedded form is scrollable; you can press Page Up or Page Down to reveal additional linked records. When the master table has a one-to-many relationship with the detail table, it is especially useful to use an embedded multi-record form.

By contrast, unlinked embedded forms are useful when there is no necessary relationship between the master table and the detail table. When you view an unlinked embedded form, any record from the detail table can be displayed. Embedded, unlinked forms are therefore scrollable and may be placed as either a single- or multi-record form. Unlinked detail tables need not be keyed.

## PREPARING EMBEDDED FORMS

Designing an embedded form for a detail table is similar to designing a normal form: you place fields, text, borders, and stylistic attributes on the form. Once you embed the form, the items on it will appear as though they are part of the multi-table form. However, the design of an embedded form must meet certain size and layout restrictions.

An embedded form must take up less space than the space alloted to a form (23 rows by 80 columns) so that it can fit on the multi-table form. Paradox considers an embedded form's size to be equal to that of a rectangle (anchored at the upper-left corner of the form-design screen) that just encloses all the fields and text on a form. Therefore, you should always design an embedded form in the upper-left corner of the form-design screen, regardless of where on the multi-table form you ultimately plan to place it.

Preparing a linked, embedded form entails additional restrictions. These relate to the structure of the master and detail tables, and the association between them. The following restrictions ensure that Paradox will be able to locate correctly the detail-table records that match the master-table record:

- An embedded form may be linked only if its table is keyed

- There must be a one-to-one or one-to-many relationship between the detail table and the master table. That is, the combination of one or more detail-table, key-field values must relate to only *one* record in the master table

- The detail-table key fields that define the link must be the first key fields in the detail table's structure

- The detail-table key fields that define the link must *not* be placed on the embedded form; all other key fields *must*, however.

## To Place an Embedded Form

1. Press F10 (Menu) from the Form mode and select Multi Tables Place.

2. Select Linked or Unlinked.

3. Enter the name of the table whose form you want to embed or press Enter to select from a menu of tables in the current directory.

4. Indicate the number of the form you are embedding from the menu.

5. If you selected Unlinked in Step 2, skip to the next step. If you selected Linked, specify which master-table fields matched each of the key fields from the detail table that were not placed on the detail-table form.

6. Use the arrow keys to move the rectangle representing the embedded form to the desired location on the multi-table form. Press Enter when you are finished.

**What For?** Once a form for a detail table is designed, you can embed it onto a multi-table form for a master table while you are designing or changing the multi-table form.

## To Remove an Embedded Form

1. Press F10 (Menu) from the Form mode and select Multi Tables Remove.

2. Move the cursor onto the embedded form you want to remove and press Enter. Paradox will prompt you to confirm your request.

3. Select Yes to remove it or No to cancel.

## To Move an Embedded Form

1. Press F10 (Menu) from the Form mode and select Multi Tables Move.

2. Move the cursor onto the embedded form you want to move and press Enter.

3. Use the arrow keys to move the form to the new location and press Enter.

## To Make Part of a Multi-table Form DisplayOnly

1. Press F10 (Menu) from the Form mode and select Multi Tables DisplayOnly.

2. Select Master or Other. If you select Other, move the cursor onto the embedded form you want to make Display-Only and press Enter. Paradox will ask you to confirm that you want to do this.

3. Select Yes.

**What For?**    To display a linked or unlinked embedded form on a master table without permitting changes to records in the embedded form's table. Or, to permit changes to records in embedded tables while preventing changes to the record in the master table.

# MULTI-RECORD FORMS

You can display more than one record from a table on a form at one time. This capability is useful when you want to view more than one record at a time, as you can in table view, yet still take advantage of the features available in forms.

The following is an outline of the general steps involved in creating a multi-record form. Refer to the following sections for more detailed descriptions of the specific steps.

## To Create a Multi-record Form

1.   Place the fields, text, and stylistic attributes that make up one record. This record will be the *original record.*

2.   Press F10 (Menu) from the Form mode and select Multi Records Define. Paradox will prompt you to select a region on the form that contains (and encloses entirely) all of the fields, text, and borders you want to duplicate in the additional record(s). Figure 4.5 shows a record that has been selected.

3.   Use the arrow keys to move to one corner of a rectangle that defines the original record and press Enter.

4.   Move to the opposite corner of this rectangle and press Enter.

5.   Use ↑ and ↓ to specify the number of copies of the original record to display and press Enter. Figure 4.6 shows an example of a multi-record region.

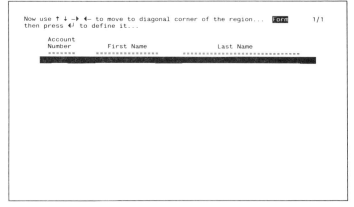

**Figure 4.5:**  A sample record, defined

The original record defines all fields, text, and attributes that will be displayed in multiple records. When designing the original record, it is important to keep in mind that copies of it will be placed below its location. Therefore, you should always leave sufficient room below the original record for them.

● **NOTE**  Multi-table forms with multi-record forms embedded in them provide a powerful means for entering data in separate yet related tables.

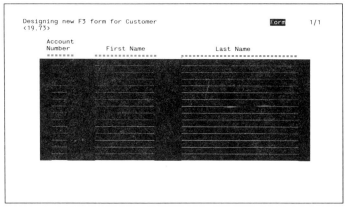

**Figure 4.6:**  A sample multi-record region

## To Remove a Multi-record Region

Press F10 (Menu) from the Form mode and select Multi
Records Remove. Paradox will delete the multi-record region
from the form, leaving the original record intact.

● **NOTE** In order to change the position of a multi-record region,
you will first need to *remove* the multi-record definition, then *move*
the original record, and then *redefine* the multi-record region.

## To Adjust the Size of a Multi-record Region

1.  Press F10 (Menu) from the Form mode and select Multi
    Records Adjust. Paradox will remove the copies of the or-
    iginal record so that you can redefine the size of the orig-
    inal record.

2.  Adjust the size of the original record with the arrow keys
    and press Enter.

3.  Use ↑ and ↓ to indicate the number of additional copies of
    the original record to display and press Enter.

**What For?** To adjust the size of a multi-record region so that it
displays either more or fewer records.

## Chapter Five

# DESIGNING REPORTS

Each table may have up to 15 reports associated with it: the standard report that Paradox automatically creates (called R) and fourteen custom-designed reports. Reports can include fields from a table, stylistic features such as borders, and text—as well as summary calculations based on groups of records from a table. You can also incorporate data from more than one table in a single report.

# TYPES OF REPORTS

Paradox produces two types of reports: tabular and free-form. Both have characteristics that make them appropriate for specific purposes.

**Tabular reports** follow the basic organization of a table. Typically, each record is displayed on a single line of a report, with fields being displayed as columns. Tabular reports are appropriate for most reporting situations in which they serve as a table or list. An example of a default tabular report-specification screen is shown in Figure 5.1.

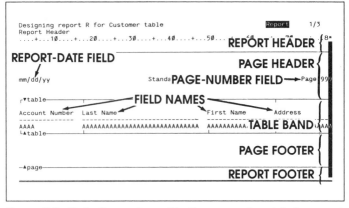

**Figure 5.1:** Default report-specification screen for a tabular report

There is less structure to a **free-form report** than the row-column orientation imposed by the tabular-report format. In free-form reports, fields for a single record often appear on more than one line. Free-form reports permit the intermixing of literal text and placed fields. An example of a default free-form report-specification screen is shown in Figure 5.2.

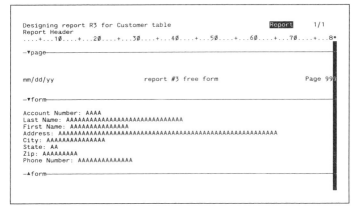

```
Designing report R3 for Customer table                    Report     1/1
Report Header
....+...1Ø....+...2Ø....+...3Ø....+...4Ø....+...5Ø....+...6Ø....+...7Ø....+...8■

─▼page───────────────────────────────────────────────────────────────────


mm/dd/yy                       report #3 free form                 Page 99Ø

─▼form────────────────────────────────────────────────────────────────────

Account Number: AAAA
Last Name: AAAAAAAAAAAAAAAAAAAAAAAAAAAAAAAA
First Name: AAAAAAAAAAAAAAA
Address: AAAAAAAAAAAAAAAAAAAAAAAAAAAAAAAAAAAAAAAAAAAAAAAAAAAAAAAAAA
City: AAAAAAAAAAAAAAA
State: AA
Zip: AAAAAAAAA
Phone Number: AAAAAAAAAAAAAA

─▲form────────────────────────────────────────────────────────────────────
```

**Figure 5.2:** Default report-specification screen for a free-form report

# DESIGNING AND CHANGING REPORTS

When you first design a report for a table, Paradox automatically includes *all* the fields from that table. Often you will want to make changes to this default design, including adding text, adding bands, placing calculated or summary fields, or removing unwanted fields.

## To Design a Report

1. Press F10 (Menu) from the Main mode and select Report Design.

2. Enter the name of the table for which you want to design the report, or press Enter and select a name from the list of tables in the current directory.

3. Select a number for the report, 1 through 14. (You can select R to redesign the standard report.)

4.  Enter a description for the report. Paradox will use it as the default report title.

5.  Select whether to design a Tabular report or a Free-form report. Paradox will display it in the default format.

6.  Make changes to the default report specification, if desired.

7.  Press F2 (Do-It!) to save the new report specification.

## To Change a Previously Designed Report

1.  Press F10 (Menu) from the Main mode and select Report Change.

2.  Enter the name of the table with which the report is associated, or press Enter and select a name from the list of tables in the current directory.

3.  Select the report you want to change from the displayed menu of reports for the table.

4.  Change the description for the report, if desired, and press Enter.

5.  Make changes to the report.

6.  Press F2 (Do-It!) to save the report specification.

Table 5.1 shows the keys you can use to move around the report-specification screen.

**Table 5.1:** Keys for the Report-Specification Screen

| Key | Effect |
| --- | --- |
| Ctrl–End | Moves cursor to the end of the rightmost field or text in a line |
| Ctrl–Home | Moves cursor to the beginning of the current line |
| Ctrl–← | Scrolls screen to the left |

**Table 5.1:** Keys for the Report-Specification Screen (continued)

| Key | Effect |
| --- | --- |
| Ctrl–R | Rotates columns in the table band of a tabular report |
| Ctrl–→ | Scrolls screen to the right |
| Ctrl–V | Displays a vertical ruler |
| Ctrl–Y | Deletes characters from the cursor to the end of the line; from the beginning of the line, deletes the entire line |
| Del | Deletes character at the cursor |
| ↓ | Moves cursor down one line |
| End | Moves cursor to the last line in a report |
| Enter | In insert mode, inserts a new line; in typeover mode, moves down one line |
| Home | Moves cursor to the first line in a report |
| Ins | Toggles between insert and typeover modes |
| ← | Moves cursor to the left |
| Page Down | Moves cursor down one half-screen |
| Page Up | Moves cursor up one half-screen |
| → | Moves cursor to the right |
| ↑ | Moves up one line |
| Alt–F7 (Instant Report) | Prints the current report |
| F10 (Menu) | Displays the Report menu |

# WORKING WITH REPORT BANDS

Reports are organized as a series of *nested bands,* each of which has a header and footer. There are four types of bands. From outermost to innermost, they are report bands, page bands, group bands, and table or form bands. These bands are said to be nested because the inner bands lie completely within the outer bands.

The **report band** is used to display fields and text at the front and back of the report. Any text and/or fields displayed on the report header appear once, at the front of the report. Any text and/or fields placed on the report footer appear once, on the last page(s) of the report. The report header can be used as a title page or cover sheet for the report. The report footer is an ideal location for overall summary fields.

The **page band** defines the top and bottom margins for each page. The page-band header and footer are printed at the top and bottom, respectively.

Unlike the other bands, **group bands** do not automatically appear on a report. You place them on a report in order to organize records based on one or more fields in a table. Information placed in a group header is displayed at the beginning of each new group while information placed in a group footer is displayed at the end of each group. A report can have as many as 16 groups, or none.

In a tabular report the innermost band is called the **table band**. In a free-form report it is called the **form band**. Information in a table or form band it printed once per record, with the exception of header information in a tabular report, which is printed once per page or group, depending on the tabular-report format.

**See Also**    *Report Settings* (this chapter).

# THE REPORT MENU

When you press F10 (Menu) while designing or changing a report, Paradox will display the Report menu. The menu options and their uses are as follows:

**Field:** Places or modifies fields in a report

**TableBand:** Inserts or modifies columns in a tabular report

**Group:** Inserts and modifies groups in a report

**Output:** Sends a report to either a monitor, printer, or disk file

**Settings:** Removes blanks and produces mailing labels in free-form reports, controls format and group repeats in tabular reports, and defines page layout and printer setups in either report format

**Help:** Displays help information for reports

**DO-IT!:** Saves a report and returns to the Main menu

**Cancel:** Cancels all changes to a report

# PLACING A FIELD

Paradox reports support seven types of fields: Regular, Summary, Calculated, Date, Time, Page, and #Record. You can include some or all of them in a report, and as many times as desired.

## To Place a Field

**1.** Press F10 (Menu) from the Report mode and select Field Place.

**2.** Select Regular, Summary, Calculated, Date, Time, Page, or #Record.

**3.** If you are placing a calculated field or a summary of a calculated field, enter the expression for the calculation. If you are placing a date field, select a date format.

**4.** Move the cursor to the position where you want the leftmost side of the field to begin and press Enter.

**5.** If the field is a date field, you are done. If the field is an alphanumeric field, use the →, ←, and Home keys to define the size of the field and press Enter. If the field is a numeric, short numeric, or currency field, use →, ←, and Home to define the number of digits to display for the field and press Enter. For numeric and currency fields, you must then define the number of decimal places to display. Use →, ←, and Home to define the number of decimal places to display and press Enter.

## TYPES OF FIELDS

**Regular fields** are fields from the table for which you are designing a report, or fields from linked tables. When you select Regular, Paradox will display a list of all regular fields. Select the field to place from this list. If you have linked the report to another lookup table, the name of that table, followed by the –> character combination, will appear at the end of the list. To place a regular field from a linked lookup table, select the table name. Paradox will then display a list of all the regular fields from the linked-lookup table. Select the desired field from this list.

A **Summary field** calculates statistics across records based on either a field value or a calculation. When it is placed in the report footer, it calculates statistics for the entire report table. When it is placed in either the page footer or group footer, you can display the value on the reports PerGroup, or Overall. A summary field placed Per-Group will display the summary statistic based on each group (or page if placed in the page footer). A summary field placed Overall will contain statistics based on all records printed up to the point where the summary field appears in the report (a cumulative statistic). Table 5.2 contains a list of the summary field options that can be placed for each data type. When you place a summary field, you can base it on a regular field or a calculated field. If you select Calculated, you must provide a valid expression. The type of summary

**Table 5.2:** Summary Fields

| Type | Summary-Field Options |
|------|----------------------|
| Alphanumeric | Count, High, Low |
| Date | Count, High, Low |
| Numeric | Sum, Average, Count, High, Low |
| Short numeric | Sum, Average, Count, High, Low |
| Currency | Sum, Average, Count, High, Low |

statistics you can place for a calculated field depends on the type of the expression.

A **Calculated field** allows you to display information on a report that is not actually stored in a table. The expression in a calculated field can include field specifiers, constants, arithmetic operators, PAL variables, and certain PAL functions. Regular field values are used in an expression by using field specifiers, enclosing the field name in square brackets. For example, a field called First Name would be specified as [First Name].

When you have linked a report to another table, you can include fields from the linked table in the expression. When doing this, you must enter field specifiers that reference both the table and field name, and separate the two by the –> character combination. For example, to include the field [Amount due] from a lookup table called Accounts, you would enter **[Accounts–>Amount Due]**.

There are three different types of calculated fields: alphanumeric, numeric, and date. Alphanumeric expressions can only use the + operator to concatenate alphanumeric fields, constants, or functions. Numeric operators can use +, –, *, and / for addition, subtraction, multiplication, and division, respectively. Date expressions can use + and – to perform date arithmetic.

Alphanumeric constants included in an expression must be enclosed in double quotes. Numeric and date constants are entered without quotation marks. Any variable defined by a PAL script (including a MiniScript) can be included in an expression, or even as the argument of a PAL function. It is not necessary for the variable to be defined when the calculated field is placed on the report, but it must be defined when you output the report. An expression can be up to 175 characters in length. Examples of valid expressions are shown in Table 5.3.

**Table 5.3:** Examples of Expressions for Calculated Fields

| Expression | Expression Type |
|---|---|
| [First Name]+" "+[Last Name] | Alphanumeric |
| "Date due:  "+STRVAL([Due Date]) | Alphanumeric |
| FORMAT("W20,AC",[Comment]) | Alphanumeric |
| [Invoice Date]+30 | Date |
| [Total price]*taxrate | Numeric (*taxrate* is a PAL variable) |

The four remaining field types are used to display information specific to a report: Date, Time, Page, and #Record. The Date and Time fields are used to display the date and time (from your computer's internal clock). Page displays the current report's page number. #Record numbers fields sequentially as you output them, either Overall or PerGroup.

**See Also**    *PAL Functions in Forms and Reports* (Appendix A).

## USING SUMMARY OPERATORS IN CALCULATIONS

You can use summary operators to calculate simple statistics across records. The summary operators are Sum, Average, Count, Min, and Max; they are used to calculate the total, average, frequency, minimum, and maximum, respectively, of a group of data. Summary operators in calculated fields are invaluable when you want to display a statistic that includes an arithmetic operation on values that are themselves statistics. One example of this is a weighted average. To produce a weighted-average price you would use the following calculation:

Sum([Quantity]*[Price])/Sum([Quantity])

Here the products of the records under the *Quantity* and *Price* fields are summed before being divided by the sum of the *Quantity* records. To perform this calculation in a group, enter the keyword **group** after the field specifiers, separating the two with a comma. For example, the above expression by group would be represented as:

Sum([Quantity]*[Price],group)/Sum([Quantity],group)

# CHANGING A FIELD

Any field on your report can be changed, including erasing a field, changing the width of a field, changing the default justifications of a field, changing the format characteristics of a field, or wordwrapping a field.

## To Erase an Existing Field

1. Press F10 (Menu) from the Report mode and select Field Erase.

2. Move the cursor to the desired field and press Enter.

## To Change the Format for a Field

1. Press F10 (Menu) from the Report mode and select Field Reformat.

2. Move the cursor to the desired field and press Enter.

3. For alphanumeric fields, select the new field size. For date fields, select from the displayed list of date formats. For numeric, short numeric, and currency fields, select the type of formatting that you want to change. Follow the prompts displayed by Paradox to complete the format change.

● **NOTE**   The type of format changes you can make to a field depends on the field type. For numeric, short numeric, and currency fields, you can change the number of digits and decimal places, sign convention, use of commas, and international format. For date fields, you can change the format of the date display. For alphanumeric fields, you can change the width of the field. Examples of the sign convention, commas, and international formats are shown in Table 5.4.

**Table 5.4:** Formatting Settings

| Format | Data | Result |
|---|---|---|
| **Sign-Convention** | | |
| Negative Only | 3.00 | 3.00 |
| | −3.00 | −3.00 |
| ParenNegative | 3.00 | 3.00 |
| | −3.00 | (3.00) |
| AlwaysSign | 3.00 | +3.00 |
| | −3.00 | −3.00 |
| **Commas** | | |
| NoCommas | 3000 | 3000 |
| Commas | 3000 | 3,000 |
| **International** | | |
| U.S.Convention | 3.00 | 3.00 |
| InternationalConvention | 3.00 | 3,00 |

## To Change the Field Justification

1. Press F10 (Menu) from the Report mode and select Field Justify.

2. Move the cursor to the desired field and press Enter.

3. Select Left, Center, Right, or Default.

• **NOTE**    Each field placed on a report is automatically justified by default, based on its field type. Alphanumeric and date fields are left-justified while numeric, short numeric, and currency fields are right-justified.

## To CalcEdit a Field

1.  Press F10 (Menu) from the Report mode and select Field CalcEdit.

2.  Move the cursor to the calculated field and press Enter.

3.  Make changes to the calculation and press Enter. You can use Ctrl–F (Field View) or Alt–F5 (Field View) to assist you in editing a calculation.

**What For?**    To change the calculations for either a calculated field or summary-calculated field.

## To Wordwrap a Field

1.  Press F10 (Menu) from the Report mode and select Field WordWrap.

2.  Move the cursor to the field you want to wrap and press Enter.

3.  Enter the maximum number of lines for the field.

**What For?**    Sometimes the contents of an alphanumeric field are too long to display adequately on a report. When the size of a field does not permit the text to be displayed on a single line, the text can be wrapped onto additional lines, up to the maximum that you define.

# LINKING TO OTHER TABLES

You can display a regular field from another table on your table, or create a calculation using fields from other tables, by linking a report to it. In order to do so, the table you wish to link must be keyed and the combination of all the key-field values must relate to only one record in the table for which you are creating the report (i.e., a one-to-one or a many-to-one relationship).

## To Link to Another Table

1. Press F10 (Menu) from the Report mode and select Field Lookup Link.

2. Enter the name of the table you want to link to, or press Enter to select from a menu of tables in the current directory.

3. For each key field in the table to which you are linking, select the corresponding field from the table for which you are creating the report.

● **NOTE** Use the Field Lookup Relink selection to change the field(s) used to link a lookup table to a report table. Use Field Lookup Unlink to remove a link from a lookup table.

# CHANGING COLUMNS IN THE TABLEBAND

In tabular reports, all fields displayed for each record are placed within columns in the table band. The TableBand option from the Report menu allows you to change the size of these columns, erase a column, move or copy a column, or add a new column.

When you first create a tabular report, the text appears in the first three lines of the table band. This text will appear at the top of each table in the report. You can edit this text, or add lines of text, by moving the cursor to the existing text, pressing the Delete or Backspace keys to erase what you want, and typing in any new text you may have.

## To Insert a New Column

1. Press F10 (Menu) from the Report mode and select Table-Band Insert.

2. Move the cursor to the location where you want to add the column and press Enter.

## To Delete a Column

1. Press F10 (Menu) from the Report mode and select Table-Band Erase.

2. Move the cursor to the column you want to delete and press Enter.

● **NOTE**   When you delete a column, any text and/or fields appearing in that column are also deleted.

## To Change the Width of a Column

1. Press F10 (Menu) from the Report mode and select Table-Band Resize.

2. Move the cursor to the rightmost position of the column you want to resize and press Enter.

3. Press ← and → to define a new width for the column and press Enter.

**What For?**   To increase the width of any column, as long as there is room in the table band. If there is not enough room, you may have to increase the page width or add an additional page before changing the column's width. Reducing a column width also requires that you first reduce the width of any text and/or fields that lie within the column. You can only reduce a column to the width of the widest element, text, or field within it.

## To Move a Column

1. Press F10 (Menu) from the Report mode and select Table-Band Move.

2. Move the cursor to the column in the table band you want to move and press Enter.

3. Move the cursor to the position in the table band where you want to move the column and press Enter.

## To Copy a Column

1. Press F10 (Menu) from the Reports mode and select Table-Band Copy.

2. Move the cursor to the column you want to copy and press Enter.

3. Move the cursor to the location where you want to place a copy of the column and press Enter.

# USING GROUPS IN A REPORT

Group bands sort records in a table by the group's values, organize data by groups, and serve as a location for displaying summary statistics for groups. An example of a report with two group bands is shown in Figure 5.3.

Groups can be based on fields, ranges of values in a field, and numbers of records. When a field in a table contains values that define group membership, you can organize the records in a report by

Using Groups in a Report  **91**

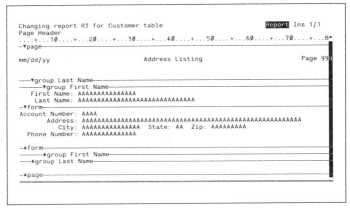

**Figure 5.3:** Group bands that sort by last and first name

grouping on that field. When you group on a field, Paradox creates one group for each unique value in the selected field.

Grouping on a range of values is useful when you want to organize records by groups of values in a field. When you select Range, Paradox asks you to select the field on which to base the range. If you select a date field, you can group the records by days, weeks, months, or years. If you select a numeric, short numeric, or currency field, Paradox will ask you to define the size of the group. For instance, if you define the size of a numeric group to be 100, Paradox will group all values from 0 to 99 in one group, 100 to 199 in a second group, and so on. If you define 10000, your groups will be 0 to 9999, 10000 to 19999, and so on. If you select an alphanumeric field, Paradox will ask you to indicate how many characters of the alphanumeric field to group. For instance, if you select 1, Paradox will group all the records whose grouped field starts with *A* in one group, *B* in another group, and so on.

Groups that are based on the number of records are useful when you want to create groups of the same size. For example, you may want to create groups that each contain 40 records. To do so, select NumberRecords as the group type and enter the number of records that you want Paradox to place in each group.

## To Place (Insert) a Group in a Report

1. Press F10 (Menu) from the Report mode and select Group Insert.

2. Select the type of group you want to insert. If you are inserting a group based on a field or a field range, you must also select the field from the displayed menu of available fields. If you are placing a group based on a field range, you must also specify the range.

3. If you are inserting a group in a report where no groups have yet been inserted, position the cursor between the table (or form) band and the page band, and press Enter. If you are adding a group to a report that already has one or more groups, move the cursor to a line inside a group, below which you want to insert the new group—or *outside* the group(s) to insert a highest-level group—and press Enter.

## To Delete a Group Band

1. Press F10 (Menu) from the Report mode and select Group Delete.

2. Move the cursor to the group band you want to delete and press Enter.

## To Modify the Display of Group Headers

1. Press F10 (Menu) from the Report mode and select Group Headings.

2. Move the cursor into the grouping band for the group whose header you want to modify and press Enter.

3. Select Group to display the headers only once per group or Page to display the headers once per group *and* at the top of each additional page on which the group is displayed.

**What For?**   When you insert a group, both text and fields in that group's header are displayed by default above the first record of each group. With this procedure, you can specify that the header should also be displayed at the top of each additional page on which the group appears. Doing so makes it easier to keep track of records that spill over several pages.

## To Change the Sort Direction of a Group

1. Press F10 (Menu) from the Report mode and select Group SortDirection.

2. Move the cursor into the group band for the group whose sort direction you want to change and press Enter.

3. Select Ascending or Descending.

**What For?** By default, a group causes records to be sorted in ascending order. Here you can define that a group be sorted in descending order.

## To Change the Type of a Group

1. Press F10 (Menu) from the Report mode and select Group Regroup.

2. Move the cursor into the group band for the group you want to change and press Enter.

3. Define a new group type.

## To Insert a Page Break in a Group Header

1. Move the cursor to the first line of the group header you want to begin on a new page.

2. Insert a new line in this header by pressing Enter while in the Insert mode.

3. Move the cursor to this new blank line and enter the word **PAGEBREAK** in the leftmost column. The word *PAGEBREAK* must appear in upper-case letters.

**What For?** Sometimes you may want a new group to always start on a new page. If you place the pagebreak command in a group header, you will make Paradox print groups on separate pages.

# OUTPUTTING A REPORT

There are two modes in Paradox from which you can output any report: Main mode and Report mode.

## To Output a Report from the Main Mode

1. Press F10 (Menu) and select Report Output.

2. Enter the name of the table that contains your report, or press Enter and select from the menu of tables in the current directory.

3. Select the number corresponding to the report you want to output.

4. Select Printer to print the report, Screen to display the report on your monitor, or File to output the report to a disk file. If you select File, you must also provide a valid DOS filename for the disk file.

## To Output a Report from the Report Mode

1. Press F10 (Menu) and select Output.

2. Select Printer to print the report, Screen to display the report on your monitor, or File to output the report to a disk file. If you select File, you must also provide a valid DOS filename for the disk file.

## To Output a Range of Pages for Your Report

1. Press F10 (Menu) from the Main mode and select Report RangeOutput.

2. Enter the name of the table that contains your report, or press Enter to select from a menu of tables in the current directory.

3. Select the number corresponding to the report you want to output.

4. Select Printer to print the report, Screen to display the report on your monitor, or File to output the report to a disk file. If you select File, you must also provide a valid DOS filename for the disk file.

5. Enter the lowest page number to output.

6. Enter the highest page number to output.

## To Print an Instant Report

Press Alt–F7 (Instant Report) from any mode. Paradox will send the standard report, R, for the current table to your printer.

**What For?**  You can use the Instant Report feature to print any Paradox table easily. It works any time a table is displayed. The instant report will be the standard report, R, that Paradox automatically generates for a table (you can redesign R if you wish).

• **NOTE**  You can also create an instant report while you are displaying the report-specification screen. In this case, the report you are designing or changing will be printed when you press Alt–F7.

# REPORT SETTINGS

You can adjust certain features of any report, including printer-setup strings, page widths and lengths, margins, and whether to pause between pages for single-sheet printing. Other features are specific to either tabular or free-form reports.

## To Use LineSqueeze

1. Press F10 (Menu) from the Report mode and select Setting RemoveBlanks LineSqueeze.

2. Select Yes to turn LineSqueeze on or No to turn it off.

3. If you select Yes, then select Fixed to output all records with the same form length or Variable to produce variable-length records.

**What For?**  LineSqueeze is used to suppress the printing of a line in a free-form report when it contains blank values. This feature is particularly useful for mailing labels and similar report styles where empty lines are undesirable. You can also specify that the records are of Variable length—or of Fixed length, in which case all blank lines are moved to the bottom of each form band when you output the report. The Fixed-setting feature is essential when you are printing on fixed-sized forms, such as mailing labels or rotary-file cards.

## To Use FieldSqueeze

1. Press F10 (Menu) from the Report mode and select Setting RemoveBlanks FieldSqueeze.

2. Select Yes to turn LineSqueeze on or No to turn it off.

**What For?**  FieldSqueeze allows you to suppress the printing of leading or trailing blanks in the fields of free-form reports. With Field-Squeeze turned on, blanks in a field are removed and all the fields and text to the right of it are moved left to compensate for the removed blanks.

## To Change the Report Format

1.  Press F10 (Menu) from the Report mode and select Setting Format.

2.  Select GroupOfTables or TableOfGroups.

**What For?** With tabular reports in which one or more group bands are used, you can set how the groups are organized. By default, tabular reports are generated as a table of groups. The table header is displayed once at the top of each page; any fields or text placed in a group header appear below it. With the Format feature, you can convert a tabular report to a group of tables. In a group of tables, the table-band header appears above each group, directly below the group header.

## To Control the Output of Repeated Groups

1.  Press F10 (Menu) from the Report mode and select Setting GroupRepeats.

2.  Select Suppress to print only the first instance of repeated, grouped fields. Select Retain to print all fields, regardless of repeats.

**What For?** When a tabular report is grouped by a field, which also appears in the table band, the values displayed in that column will be the same within each group. GroupRepeats allows you to suppress the output of these duplicate values; when it is set to Suppress, only the first record in each group will display the value.

## To Change the Length and/or Width of a Report

1.  Press F10 (Menu) from the Report mode and select Setting PageLayout.

2.  Select Width to change the width of a single page and then enter the number of columns to appear on each page. Select Length to change the page length and then enter the number of lines to appear on each page. To output a report with a continuous page length, enter the letter **C**.

# To Adjust the Number of Report Pages

1.  Press F10 (Menu) from the Report mode and select Setting PageLayout.

2.  Choose Insert to add a new page or Delete to delete an existing page. If you select Delete, Paradox will ask you to confirm the deletion.

**What For?**    A report can be more than one page wide. When you are adding fields, you may need to increase the number of report pages to accommodate them. Alternatively, after removing fields from a report you may want to erase previously added pages that are now blank.

# The Define a Left Margin

1.  Press F10 (Menu) from the Report menu and select Setting Margin.

2.  Indicate the number of characters that Paradox should reserve for the left margin and press Enter.

# To Define a Printer-Setup String

1.  Press F10 (Menu) from the Report mode and select Setting Setup.

2.  To select a predefined setup string, select Predefined and choose from the menu. To use a custom setup string, select Custom, select the port to which your printer is connected, and enter the setup string.

**What For?**    Printer-setup strings are used to control the printing features of your printer, including whether to print in standard or condensed type, or to use a portrait or landscape orientation.

● **NOTE**    Many printers require that an Esc (Escape) character be sent to the printer as part of the setup string. In Paradox, use **\027** to represent this. For example, to send an Esc–E to your printer, enter **\027E**.

**See Also**   *The Custom Configuration Program* (Chapter 1) to define new printer-setup strings or to change the default printer-setup string.

## To Create Mailing Labels

1. Design a free-form report.

2. Delete all existing lines from the report and page headers and footers.

3. Place the desired fields in the form band of the report. They should define the layout of a single mailing label.

4. Adjust the form length so that it is equal to the number of lines for a single mailing label.

5. Adjust the page width so that it is equal to the number of columns for a single mailing label.

6. If there is more than one column of mailing labels on each page, set the number of pages for the report equal to the number of columns of mailing labels. These pages should be blank; fields should be placed on page 1 only.

7. Press F10 (Menu) from the Main mode and select Setting Labels Yes.

## To Print a Report One Page at a Time

Press F10 (Menu) from the Report mode and select Setting Wait Yes.

*Chapter Six*

# QUERIES

This chapter covers Paradox queries that extract, manipulate, and analyze data stored in tables. Specifically, you can perform the following tasks:

- Select one or more fields from one or more tables

- Select only those records that meet certain criteria

- Combine information from two or more related tables

- Calculate simple statistics based on groups of records within a table

- Create new fields containing the results of calculations

- Select records based on their comparison with a specific group of records

- Change data in a table

- Insert data from one or more tables into another table

- Delete records from a table

# MAKING QUERIES

Paradox queries are defined visually using Query-By-Example (often referred to as QBE). All queries are made by means of a *query form*, such as the one shown in Figure 6.1. It contains one column for each of the fields in the corresponding table—in this case, *Account Number, Last Name, First Name,* and *Address*—as well as an additional field called the *table field* that is labeled with the table's name—*CUSTOMER* in the figure. The table field is always the left-most field in a query form.

Constructing a query involves placing check marks, conditions, examples, key words, and calculations on one or more fields of a query form. You can include more than one condition, example, or calculation in any field by separating them with commas.

A query may involve more than one table. However, each table can be represented by only one query form. All query forms displayed on the workspace must be involved in the query. You can move among the different query forms on the workspace with the F3 (Up Image) and F4 (Down Image) keys.

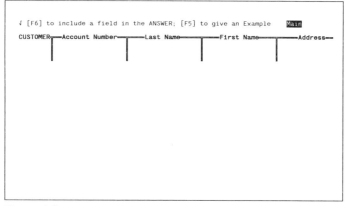

**Figure 6.1:** A query form

## To Make a Query

**1.** Press F10 (Menu) from the Main mode and select Ask.

**2.** Enter the name of the table you want to query, or press Enter and select from a menu of tables in the current directory. If more than one table is involved in the query, repeat this step until all required query forms are displayed.

**3.** Construct the query as described in this chapter.

**4.** Press F2 (Do-It!) to initiate the query.

When you initiate a query, Paradox evaluates whether it makes sense and, if so, processes it. Paradox selects records from the queried table(s) that meet the criteria specified in all fields of the query form and places them in a temporary table called Answer, which will also include the results of any calculations or operations specified in the query.

# SELECTING FIELDS

A field is selected from a table by placing a check (✓), check-plus (✓+), or check-descending (✓▼) indicator in the corresponding field of a query form. Each of these marks relates to a different task. The most general is Check Plus, which selects *all* values from a field in the queried table. Check, on the other hand, selects only *one* instance of each value in a field. When two or more fields are checked in a query, the Answer table will contain unique combinations of values from the checked fields. In addition, Check sorts the Answer table in ascending order based on the checked fields. Check Descending is similar to Check, except that it sorts the Answer-table records in descending order. All three types of checks can be used together in the same query, as long as each relates to its own field.

## To Select a Field from a Table

1. While in the Main mode, move to the desired field in the query form.

2. Press F6 (Check), Alt–F6 (Check Plus), or Ctrl–F6 (Check Descending) to place the desired indicator in the field.

## To Select All Fields from a Table

1. While in the Main mode, move to the table field (the leftmost field) in the query form.

2. Press F6 (Check), Alt–F6 (Check Plus), or Ctrl–F6 (Check Descending) to place the desired indicator in all fields.

## To Deselect a Field

1. While in the Main mode, move the cursor to the field containing the indicator.

2. Press F6 (Check), Alt–F6 (Check Plus) or Ctrl–F6 (Check Descending) to toggle any indicator off.

# SELECTING RECORDS

You can select a specific subset of records from a queried table by defining conditions that the records must meet in order to be chosen. One or more conditions can be placed in a field to define the subset of records you want to select. If no records in the queried table match the condition(s) you specify, the Answer table will be empty.

## To Define an Exact Match

1. Move the cursor to the desired field.

2. Enter the value to match.

**3.** Repeat Steps 1 and 2 to place values in other fields.

For instance, to select all customers from a table whose last name is Jones, you can type **Jones** in the Last Name field of the Customer query form shown in Figure 6.1. The exact spelling and capitalization entered will be matched.

## To Define a Range of Values

Use the comparison operators shown in Table 6.1, followed by a value.

For example, if you have a table that contains a date field, and you want to select only those records that fall after 1 August 1991, enter the condition **>8/1/91** in the date field. To select records dated 1 August 1991 or earlier, enter the range **<=8/1/91**. You can include two or more range conditions for the same field, as long as they are separated by commas. For example, to select records with any date during August 1991, enter **>=8/1/91, <9/1/91**.

## To Select Records with Arithmetic Operators

Use the arithmetic operators shown in Table 6.2 with constants, PAL variables, example elements, and/or special operators to define the condition.

**What For?** Including an arithmetic operator in a condition provides you with a tremendous amount of flexibility if you work with PAL variables or example elements that link to other tables. For example, if the example element PRICE refers to the price of a certain

**Table 6.1**: Comparison Operators

| Operator | Description |
|----------|-------------|
| = | Equal to |
| > | Greater than |
| < | Less than |
| >= | Greater than or equal to |
| <= | Less than or equal to |

**Table 6.2**: Arithmetic Operators

| Operator | Valid Field Type |
|----------|------------------|
| +        | Alphanumeric, Date, Numeric |
| −        | Date, Numeric |
| /        | Numeric |
| *        | Numeric |

product, the condition PRICE*2 will select all records whose value equals twice the amount referred to by PRICE.

Alphanumeric constants must be enclosed in quotation marks. PAL variables must be preceded by the tilde (~) character. You cannot mix value types (alphanumeric, date, or numeric) within a single arithmetic expression.

**See Also**    *Querying Field Values* (this chapter).

# SPECIAL OPERATORS IN QUERIES

Paradox has a number of special operators you can use in queries:

**Blank**: Use the Blank operator to refer to values in a field that are not defined. For example, to select all records whose date field is blank, check the appropriate field(s) and enter **BLANK** in the date field.

**Like**: When you do not know the exact value for a condition, use the Like operator to process records whose field contents are similar to a condition. For instance, enter **LIKE Smith** in the Last Name field of a query form to select records where the last name is similar to *Smith,* such as *Smithe* and *Smyth.*

@ and .. : When the Like operator is unpredictable, use these pattern operators to select records with similar values more precisely. The at sign (@) represents just one character of any type, and double periods (..) represent zero, one, or more characters of any type. When a pattern operator is used in a condition, upper- and lowercase letters are treated equally.

**Not** : Use the Not operator to select all records that do not match the condition defined for a field. For example, if you enter **NOT 9/1/91** in a date field of a query form, Paradox will select all records except those dated 9/1/91.

**Or** : The Or operator is a logic operator that allows you to select records that meet one or more conditions in the same field. If at least one of the conditions is met (and any conditions placed on other fields are also met), the record will be selected. For example, to select all records for dates earlier than 9/1/91 as well as records where the date is later than 1/1/92, specify the condition **<9/1/91 OR >1/1/92**.

**,** : The And operator (,) allows you to include more than one condition, example, or calculation in any one field. When you separate conditions with a comma, *all* conditions specified must be met for that field in order for a record to be selected.

**As** : The As operator is used for naming fields in the Answer table. It is appropriate only when a field is checked with one of the three indicators, or when a calculation is defined for a field that will create a new field in the Answer table. For example, entering the condition **>9/1/91 AS Future Dates** in a date field that is checked will create a field in the Answer table named Future Date that contains the selected values.

**Today** : The Today operator represents the current date as defined by your computer's internal clock. For instance, to select all records whose date is equal to today's date, enter **TODAY** in the date field.

● **NOTE**   Any time that conditions or expressions include a word that is also a query operator keyword, it must be enclosed in quotation marks. For instance, if you want to create a query that selects all customers who reside in Oregon, and the state field in your table uses two-letter state codes, you must enclose the state code for Oregon in quotation marks: **"OR"**. Without them, Paradox would treat **OR** as the Or operator instead.

To define a condition that contains quotation marks itself, precede each one with a backslash (\). A backslash tells Paradox to take the next character literally (this is also useful for conditions that include commas). For instance, to select the name Robert "Bob" Davis for a field, enter **Robert \"Bob\" Davis**.

## CREATING AN OR QUERY WITHOUT THE OR OPERATOR

Although the Or operator can be used to create Or queries when two or more conditions are defined for a *single* field, Or queries become somewhat more complicated when they relate to two or more fields. The following conditions must be met to construct an Or query involving multiple fields:

- Each of the Or conditions must be placed on a separate line of the query form

- Check marks must be placed in all lines of the query form for each field that is checked

Figure 6.2 displays a query and the resulting Answer table, which contains customers whose first name is Jane or last name is Smith.

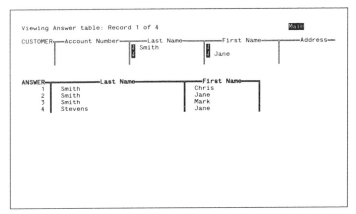

**Figure 6.2:** Query and resulting Answer table

# QUERYING FIELD VALUES

You can refer to the values stored in a field during a query. The two most common situations for doing this are using field values in a calculation (such as adding 10 percent to the price of all products listed in a product table) and using values in one table as the condition for selecting records in another table. (This is how you link two or more tables in a query.) You use an *example element* to refer to field values. Paradox distinguishes between the example element and other text in a query by displaying it in reverse video. Once you have defined an example element for a field, you may use it in calculations, expressions, and conditions.

## To Define an Example Element

1.  From the Main mode, move the cursor to the field for which you want to define an example element and press F5 (Example).

2.  Type one or more characters to define it. It may consist of only letters (A–Z) or numerals (0–9).

## PERFORMING CALCULATIONS IN QUERIES

You can perform calculations in queries and place the results in a field in the Answer table. There are two types of calculations available in Paradox. The first type uses constants, field values represented by example elements, and PAL variables. The second type uses *summary operators* to calculate statistics based on groups of records.

## To Define a Calculation Involving Field Values

1.  From the Main mode, place an example element in each of the fields that will be involved in the calculation.

**2.** In any field in the query, enter the keyword **CALC** followed by the calculation, which can include constants, PAL variables, and example elements. PAL variables must be preceded by a tilde (~) character.

**What For?**   Calculations in queries allow you to add a field to the Answer table that contains the result of the calculation. When you define this type of calculation, it can be placed in any field of the query form (except the table field). An example of a query involving a calculation, and the resulting Answer table, is shown in Figure 6.3.

● **NOTE**   It is not mandatory that this type of calculation involve field values (example elements). However, *not* including them necessarily means that the calculated field in the Answer table will contain the same value for every record—i.e., the calculation will result in a constant.

```
√ [F6] to include a field in the ANSWER; [F5] to give an Example    Main —▼
 INDETAIL┬Invoice #┬Product Code┬─────Quantity────┬────Unit price─
         │    ✓    │     ✓      │✓ quant, calc quant * price│✓ price
```

```
 ANSWER─Invoice #┬Product Code┬Quantity─┬─Unit price─┬Quantity * Unit price┐
      1 │  1000  │   6200     │    3    │   207.90   │        623.70       │
      2 │  1000  │   7500     │    1    │   199.00   │        199.00       │
      3 │  1001  │   2000     │    5    │   795.00   │      3,975.00       │
      4 │  1001  │   3000     │    1    │   219.00   │        219.00       │
      5 │  1002  │   4200     │    1    │   149.00   │        149.00       │
      6 │  1003  │   3000     │    2    │   219.00   │        438.00       │
      7 │  1003  │   4200     │    4    │   149.00   │        596.00       │
      8 │  1004  │   2000     │    1    │   795.00   │        795.00       │
      9 │  1005  │   3000     │    1    │   219.00   │        219.00       │
     10 │  1005  │   4200     │    2    │   149.00   │        298.00       │
     11 │  1006  │   6200     │    2    │   189.00   │        378.00       │
     12 │  1007  │   7500     │    1    │   199.00   │        199.00       │
     13 │  1008  │   2000     │    1    │   795.00   │        795.00       │
     14 │  1008  │   3000     │    1    │   219.00   │        219.00       │
     15 │  1009  │   7500     │    2    │   199.00   │        398.00       │
     16 │  1010  │   2000     │    1    │   795.00   │        795.00       │
```

**Figure 6.3:** Query involving a calculation and the resulting Answer table

# QUERIES OF TWO OR MORE TABLES

To query more than one table, you link tables based on related fields with one or more example elements. Paradox links the tables together by matching the values from each of their fields that have the same example element entered in the different query forms.

Once example elements link tables together, the tables are treated for querying purposes as though they were a single table. That is, conditions may be placed in any of the linked tables to define which records will be processed. Also, check marks can be used on any of the linked tables to select fields or group records. An example of a two-table query is shown in Figure 6.4.

## To Link Tables

1.   From the Main mode, display query forms on the workspace for at least two related tables.

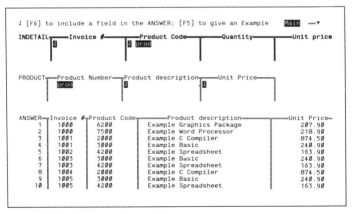

**Figure 6.4:** A query of two tables

**2.** Place the same example element in each set of fields on which you want to base the link.

# THE INCLUSION OPERATOR

When two tables are linked together by a single field in a query, only those records that contain matching values in two linked fields are processed. This is called an *inner join*. The inclusion operator (!) allows you to select records from one or both tables, even when there is no match in the linked tables. When the inclusion operator is defined for only *one* of the tables, the join is called an *asymmetrical outer join*. When the inclusion operator is defined for *both* tables, the join is called a *symmetrical outer join*.

## To Use the Inclusion Operator

Append the example element for the table whose records you want to include (regardless of a match to the linked table) with an exclamation mark (!).

An example of an asymmetrical outer join is shown in Figure 6.5. Here at least one record appears in the Answer table for each

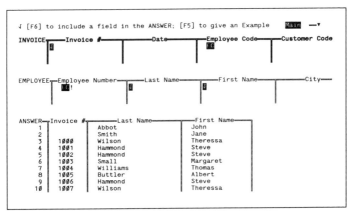

**Figure 6.5:** An asymmetrical outer join

employee, whether or not he or she accounted for a sale listed in the Invoice table. If this same query made use of the inclusion operator for both example elements that link the Invoice table to the Employee table (i.e., a symmetrical outer join), the Answer table would show records of employees who (a) do not appear in the Employee table, (b) do not appear in the Invoice table, and (c) appear in both.

Below are some important facts about the inclusion operator:

- Although inner and outer joins can both be used in the same query, any two lines in a query can be linked by either inner joins or outer joins, but not both

- The inclusion operator can be used no more than twice for the same example element in a query

- Paradox processes inner joins before asymmetrical outer joins. Symmetrical outer joins are processed last

# USING GROUPS IN QUERIES

Check and Check Descending both select fields and group records based on field values. This allows you to extract information about groups of data in a table.

## To Identify Groups of Values in a Field

1. Move to the field in a query form for which you want to group records and press F6 (Check) or Ctrl–F6 (Check Descending) from the Main mode.

2. Repeat Step 1 to perform additional groupings.

## SELECTING RECORDS WITH SUMMARY OPERATORS

Summary operators allow you to select records that satisfy a statistical criterion. For instance, to select records whose average in a field is greater than 100, enter the condition **AVERAGE>100**. (At least one other field in the query must contain a Check or Check Descending to define the group.)

There are five summary operators (see Table 6.3). SUM and AVERAGE consider all values in a field, while COUNT, MIN, and MAX consider only unique values. You can control this feature by using the keywords ALL or UNIQUE. For example, to select a group of records for which the sum of unique sales exceeded 1000 units, you would place a Check or Check Descending in the field which defines the group and enter the condition **SUM UNIQUE>1000** in the field representing unit sales.

Summary operators can also be used to calculate statistics for each group. This is done by entering the keyword **CALC** followed by the statistic you want to calculate. To calculate the sum of a field, for example, enter **CALC SUM** in the corresponding field in the query form. To calculate statistics by groups, add a Check or a Check Descending to the field by which you want to group the statistics.

The UNIQUE and ALL keywords can also be used in calculations. For instance, to modify **CALC COUNT** so that it counts *all* records, regardless of duplicate values, you would enter **CALC COUNT ALL**.

## To Calculate Group Statistics

1. Place a Check or Check Descending in each of the grouping fields, from the Main mode, to calculate statistics for groups within the table. Do not use any check marks to calculate statistics for an entire table.

2. For each field in which you want to calculate statistics, enter **CALC** followed by the appropriate summary operator and optional keyword **UNIQUE** or **ALL**.

**Table 6.3:** Summary Operators

| Summary | Default | Description |
|---------|---------|-------------|
| Average | All | Average value (arithmetic mean) of records within each group |
| Count | Unique | Number of instances of records within each group |
| Min | Unique | Minimum value of records within each group |
| Max | Unique | Maximum value of records within each group |
| Sum | All | Total of record values within each group |

## THE ONLY OPERATOR

The Only operator is used to select groups that match a specific condition, and no other. For example, to select the customers who have never ordered more than one of any product, use a check mark to group by individual customer and then enter **ONLY 1** in the field representing the number of units ordered.

# SET QUERIES

There are two types of set queries, those that use set-comparison operators and those that use summary operators. Similar principles are used to create both of these types of queries.

## To Create a Set Query

1. Define the set.

2. Construct the comparison to the set.

3. Link additional tables, if desired.

**What For?**   Set queries allow you to compare a set of records with other records or groups of records. For example, you can define customers from one city as a set and then compare the other customers in your database with those in the set.

## To Define a Set

1. Display the query form on the workspace.

2. Enter the word **SET** in the table field on each line of the query that is involved in the set definition.

3. Enter an example element in the field whose values define the set (this is usually a key field). Enter this example element in the fields where you would normally place a check mark to produce one record for each member of the set.

4. Optionally, enter one or more conditions that restrict the set to specified records. If no conditions are specified, the set will be defined to include all records in the table(s) used in the set definition.

## To Construct a Comparison to a Set

1. On a line not involved in the set definition, precede the example element used in the set definition with a set-comparison operator or a summary operator.

2. Place at least one check mark on this same line to define the group that will be compared to the set

3. Place a check mark in any additional field(s) you want to extract and have placed in the Answer table.

There are four set-comparison operators:

   **Only**: Selects groups that only contain records defined by a set

   **No**: Selects groups that contain no records that are members of a set

**Every**: Selects groups that contain at least one instance of every member of a set

**Exactly**: A combination of Every and Only, it selects groups that contain at least one instance of every member of a set and no members that are not part of a set

Figure 6.6 displays a set query that uses the set-comparison operator called Every. The set is defined as customers whose mailing addresses are in Houston. The group is defined as employees. This set query produces an Answer table that contains the employee code for each employee who has made a sale to every customer living in Houston.

Summary comparisons allow you to compare records to summary values based on a defined set. There are five summary operators:

**Average**: Averages (arithmetic mean) record values within each group

**Count**: Counts the number of instances of records within each group

**Max**: Displays maximum value of records within each group

**Min**: Displays minimum value of records within each group

**Sum**: Totals record values within each group

On the summary-comparison line of the query, one of the summary operators is preceded by a *range operator* and followed by the example.

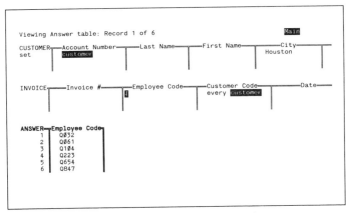

**Figure 6.6:** A set query using the Every comparison operator

Refer to Table 6.1 for a list of these operators. An example of a set query with the Average operator is shown in Figure 6.7.

Summary operators can also appear on the left-hand side of the range operator. This technique allows you to compare summary values from groups to the summary value based on a set.

## To Group without Check Marks

1. Move to the field in the query form by which you want to group.

2. Press Shift–F6 (GroupBy). Paradox places a **G** in the field.

**What For?** Instead of using a check mark as a grouping operator to define how the data you want to compare are grouped, you can use the grouping operator called GroupBy. GroupBy differs from the check mark in that it does not result in the addition of a field to the Answer table.

● **NOTE** GroupBy can only be used in set-comparison queries and only on the same line in which one of the four set-comparison operators appears.

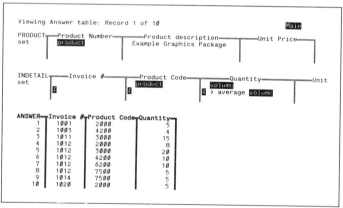

**Figure 6.7:** Set query using the Average operator

# QUERY OPERATIONS

There are four query operations, three of which allow you to manipulate tables—Delete, Insert, and Changeto. As a result of each of
these queries, Paradox creates a temporary table; it does not necessarily make an Answer table. These tables are called Deleted, Inserted, and Changed; they contain records from the queried table
that are respectively deleted, inserted, or changed. Once the query
is processed, the temporary table is displayed on the workspace as
the current table. You can then examine the deleted, inserted, or
changed records to determine whether the query produced the
desired result. If not, use the Deleted, Inserted, or Changed table to
restore your original table.

The fourth query operation, Find, allows you to locate one or more
records in a table based on values in one or more fields. Unlike
the other three query operations, a Find query does not change the
queried table.

**See Also**    *Adding, Subtracting, and Emptying Tables* (Chapter 8) on
how to add two tables and subtract one table's records from another.

## To Delete Some or All Records from a Table

1.  From the Main mode, enter the keyword **DELETE** in the
    table field of the query form for the table from which you
    want to delete records.

2.  Use conditions or example elements from other tables to
    define the records to delete. If you do not specify any con-
    ditions, Paradox will delete all records from the table.

## To Add Data to a Table

1.  From the Main mode, display two or more query forms on
    the workspace.

2.  Enter the keyword **INSERT** in the table field that cor-
    responds to the table to which you want to insert records.

**3.** Use examples to link the field(s) in the table you are inserting from to the field(s) in the table you are inserting to.

**4.** Use conditions to define which data to insert, if you wish.

## To Change Field Values in a Query

**1.** From the Main mode, move to the field in the query form whose corresponding field values you want to change.

**2.** Enter the keyword **CHANGETO** followed by a valid expression that defines the new contents of the field.

**3.** If you wish, use conditions to define which records to change.

**What For?** The Changeto query modifies the contents of one or more fields. You can use the field value itself in the Changeto expression by using example elements. Figure 6.8, for example, shows how all product prices can be increased 10 percent by multiplying the price by 1.1.

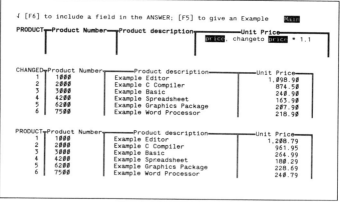

**Figure 6.8:** A Changeto query

## To Find Records in a Table

1.  Enter the keyword **FIND** in the table field of the query form.

2.  Enter one or more conditions that define the record(s) you want to find.

**What For?**  The Find query locates a record based on one or more field values. It creates an Answer table which contains *all* records that match the conditions. This table, however, is not automatically displayed once the query is processed.

# SAVING QUERIES

Once you have defined a query on the workspace, you can save it for use at a later time (whether or not you have processed it yet). When you save a query, Paradox creates a PAL script based on the query image.

## To Save a Query

1.  With the desired query displayed, press F10 (Menu) from the Main mode and select Scripts QuerySave.

2.  Enter a name for the saved query. This name must conform to the same rules for naming a table.

## To Restore a Saved Query

1.  Remove any query forms currently on the workspace by (a) making them current with the F3 (Up Image) and F4 (Down Image) keys and (b) pressing F8 (Clear Image).

2.  Press F10 (Menu) from the Main mode and select Scripts Play.

3. Enter the name of the script that contains the saved query or press Enter and select from the menu of scripts in the current directory. Paradox re-creates the query on the workspace.

4. If desired, make changes to the displayed query.

5. Press F2 (Do-It!) to process the query.

## To Speed Up a Query

Press F10 (Menu) from the Main mode and select Scripts Query-Speed. (A query must first be present on the workspace.)

**What For?**   A query that involves key fields is processed faster than one that does not. When you construct a query without key fields, you can use the QuerySpeed feature to improve processing speed. This feature (called QuerySpeedup in Paradox 3.0 and earlier) creates secondary indices that are then used to produce faster query results. If no speedup is possible, Paradox will display a message indicating this.

*Chapter Seven*

# CREATING
# CROSSTABS AND GRAPHS

This chapter describes crosstabs and graphs. Crosstabs allow you to summarize data stored in tables. Paradox's presentation-style graph feature allows you to create many different graphs of data stored in tables.

# CROSSTABS

The term *crosstab* is short for *cross-tabulation,* a procedure for summarizing data. A crosstab can make it easier to analyze and identify relationships between data from two or more fields, since it displays summary values. It can also provide a convenient way to prepare data for reports or graphs since you often want to display summary values in a graph.

When you perform a crosstab, Paradox places the results in a temporary table called Crosstab. Figure 7.1 shows an example of the Crosstab table that is created when a crosstab is performed on the original table.

The Product field from the original table is sorted into groups that become the row labels of the Crosstab table. The Salesperson field is sorted into groups that become the column labels of the Crosstab table. The Total-sale field is summarized for each row/column combination, so that the dollar amounts appear in the cells of the Crosstab table. You can also include more than one field in the row labels. Figure 7.2, for example, shows a Crosstab table in which two

```
Viewing Crosstab table: Record 1 of 10                    Main  ▲──

SALES──────┬─Product────┬─Disk type─┬─Salesperson─┬──Total sale─
    14     │Word Processor│  3 1/2   │  Al Acer    │   1,592.00
    15     │Database      │  3 1/2   │  Diane Dent │   1,197.00
    16     │Assembler     │  Both    │  Diane Dent │   1,290.00
    17     │Word Processor│  5 1/4   │  Bea Burns  │   1,592.00
    18     │Spreadsheet   │  3 1/2   │  Al Acer    │   3,990.00
    19     │Assembler     │  Both    │  Bea Burns  │   1,290.00
    20     │Fast Basic    │  Both    │  Al Acer    │      99.00
    21     │Game          │  Both    │  Al Acer    │      29.00
    22     │Assembler     │  Both    │  Diane Dent │     129.00


CROSSTAB──┬────Product────┬───Al Acer──┬───Bea Burns──┬───Chris Coo──
    1     │Assembler      │  5,160.00  │   9,030.00   │   5,160.00
    2     │C Compiler     │  4,158.00  │   6,138.00   │   6,435.00
    3     │DOS Shell      │  1,287.00  │   1,482.00   │   1,911.00
    4     │Database       │ 11,172.00  │  19,551.00   │  17,556.00
    5     │Educational    │  1,073.00  │   1,305.00   │     696.00
    6     │Fast Basic     │  1,782.00  │   3,168.00   │   3,762.00
    7     │Game           │    783.00  │   1,131.00   │   1,218.00
    8     │HD Backup      │  1,960.00  │   2,352.00   │   1,617.00
    9     │Spreadsheet    │ 19,551.00  │  20,349.00   │  10,374.00
   10     │Word Processor │  6,368.00  │   5,373.00   │   6,766.00
```

**Figure 7.1:** Original table (Sales) used in the crosstab and the resulting Crosstab table

```
Viewing Crosstab table: Record 11 of 14                    Main  ▲━━

SALES━┳Disk type━━━━━━Product━━━━━━━━Salesperson━━━┳Total sale━━┓
   15 ┃ 3 1/2    Database           Diane Dent      ┃  1,197.00  ┃
   16 ┃ Both     Assembler          Diane Dent      ┃  1,290.00  ┃
   17 ┃ 5 1/4    Word Processor     Bea Burns       ┃  1,592.00  ┃
   18 ┃ 3 1/2    Spreadsheet        Al Acer         ┃  3,990.00  ┃
   19 ┃ Both     Assembler          Bea Burns       ┃  1,290.00  ┃
   20 ┃ Both     Fast Basic         Al Acer         ┃     99.00  ┃
   21 ┃ Both     Game               Al Acer         ┃     29.00  ┃
   22 ┃ Both     Assembler          Diane Dent      ┃    129.00  ┃


CROSSTAB┳Disk type━━━━━━━Product━━━━━━━━Al Acer━━━━━━Bea Burns━━━┓
    1 ┃ 3 1/2    DOS Shell             468.00        819.00  ┃ ▪
    2 ┃ 3 1/2    Database            4,389.00     10,374.00  ┃ ▪
    3 ┃ 3 1/2    Spreadsheet         9,975.00     10,773.00  ┃ ▪
    4 ┃ 3 1/2    Word Processor      3,184.00      1,194.00  ┃ ▪
    5 ┃ 5 1/4    DOS Shell             819.00        663.00  ┃ ▪
    6 ┃ 5 1/4    Database            6,783.00      9,177.00  ┃ ▪
    7 ┃ 5 1/4    Spreadsheet         9,576.00      9,576.00  ┃ ▪
    8 ┃ 5 1/4    Word Processor      3,184.00      4,179.00  ┃ ▪
    9 ┃ Both     Assembler           5,160.00      9,030.00  ┃ ▪
   10 ┃ Both     C Compiler          4,158.00      6,138.00  ┃ ▪
   11 ┃ Both     Educational         1,073.00      1,305.00  ┃ ▪
```

**Figure 7.2:** Row labels based on two fields

fields from the original table, Product and Disk type, make the new row labels.

# TYPES OF SUMMARY CROSSTABS

You can compute the following summary statistics in a crosstab:

**Sum:** Total field values based on each row/column combination

**Min:** Minimum field values based on each row/column combination

**Max:** Maximum field values based on each row/column combination

**Count:** The number of records for each row/column combination

# To Prepare a Table for a Crosstab

Make sure that you have done the following:

- To create row labels using one field, that field must be the first (leftmost) field in the table

- To create row labels from two or more fields, the first field to be grouped (sorted on) must be the first or leftmost field

in the table, the second field to be grouped must be the
second field, and so on

•   The field whose values will be summarized, the crosstab
    value field, must contain numbers and be of either the
    field type numeric, short numeric, or currency

If the fields in the table are not in the desired order to perform a
crosstab, use Ctrl–R (Rotate) or the Main-menu selections Image
Move Field to move the desired fields into position.

## To Create a Crosstab

1.   From the Main mode, press F10 (Menu) and select Image
     Graph CrossTab.

2.   Select the type of summary statistic you want to compute
     in the crosstab: Sum, Min, Max, or Count.

3.   Press ← and → to move to the field to be used for the row
     labels in the Crosstab table and press Enter. Fields to the
     left of this field will also be used for row labels in the
     Crosstab table.

4.   Press ← and → to move to the field to be used for the
     column labels in the Crosstab table and press Enter.

5.   Press ← and → to move to the crosstab-value field (the
     field with the values you want to be summarized) and
     press Enter.

## To Create an Instant Crosstab

1.   While in the Main mode, make sure that the crosstab-
     value field is the last (rightmost) field in the table image.

2.   The column-labels field must be to the immediate left of
     the crosstab-value field.

3.   Place the cursor on the field you want to be the last row
     label in the Crosstab table.

4.   Press Alt–X.

# GRAPHS

Paradox can produce presentation-quality graphs of data stored in any table. In most cases, however, you will first perform a query or a crosstab to summarize the data in a table before generating a graph.

When you create a graph, Paradox uses the current graph settings to determine how the graph will be displayed. These settings define the many characteristics of a graph, including the graph's style, patterns, colors, and fonts. You will probably want to modify these settings before producing a final copy of the graph. If you do not modify the settings or load a .G-extension file containing previously saved graph settings, Paradox will use the default graph settings to create your graph.

You access Paradox's graphing features through the Graph menu. The Graph menu options are:

**Modify:** Modifies the current graph settings

**Load:** Loads a previously saved graph-settings file

**Save:** Saves the current graph settings to a file with the extension .G

**Reset:** Resets the graph settings to their defaults

**CrossTab:** Creates a crosstab of the current table

**ViewGraph:** Displays or prints the graph, or writes the graph settings to a disk file

## To Prepare a Table for Graphing

Consider the following restrictions:

- For unkeyed tables, the field used for the $x$-axis values must be the first (leftmost) field in the table image. Its field type can be numeric or alphanumeric for all graph types except XY graphs, which require a numeric field type

- For keyed tables, the field used for the $x$-axis values is the last (lowest level) key field. If the table has more than one

key field, the other fields will be used to determine the
order of the $x$ axis

- The field(s) used for $y$-axis values (plotted with respect to
the $y$ axis) must be a numeric field type

- The cursor must be current in the field used for the first
series plotted against the $y$ axis

- Any numeric fields (numeric, short numeric, or currency),
up to five, that appear consecutively to the immediate
right of the current field will be plotted as additional series.
If the field to the immediate right of the current field is not
a numeric field, or the current field is the last field in the
table image, Paradox will graph only one series

If the fields in the table are not in the correct order, use Ctrl–R (Rotate)
or the Main-menu selections Image Move to move the fields into the
desired positions. For keyed tables, you may want to remove the keys
for graphing purposes by selecting Modify from the Main menu and
then Sort, placing the results in a new unkeyed table.

**See Also**    Chapter 3 for information on sorting records in a table;
moving a field's display position, and using the Rotate key.

## To Create a Graph

1. Move the cursor to the field containing the first series data
(the $y$ data).

2. From the Main mode, press F10 (Menu) and select Image
Graph ViewGraph.

3. Select Screen, Printer, or File to display the graph on the
screen, output it, or write the graph to a disk file, respectively. The graph will be displayed with the current graph
settings.

● **NOTE**    In order to display a graph on your screen, your computer must be equipped with a compatible graphics adapter and
monitor. To print a graph, you must have an output device capable
of producing graphs. Before printing or plotting a graph, set up your

printer or plotter using the Graphs Printers selection in the Custom
Configuration Program (see Chapter 1).

## To Create an Instant Graph

1.  Move the cursor to the field containing the first series data
    (the *y* data).

2.  From the Main mode, press Ctrl–F7 (Instant Graph).

## To Modify the Current Graph Settings

1.  From the Main mode, press F10 (Menu) and select Image
    Graph Modify.

    Paradox will display the Customize Graph Type form
    shown in Figure 7.3.

2.  At **Graph Type** (highlighted in the Figure), type the first
    letter of the desired graph type (shown in the list on
    the right).

3.  For a combination graph, define at the highlighted list of
    **1st Series** through **6th Series** how each series is to be rep-
    resented (settings are shown in the list on the right).

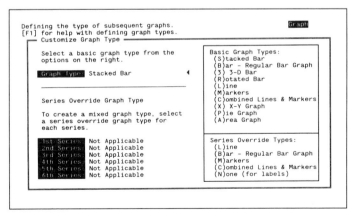

**Figure 7.3:** Customize Graph Type form

**4.**   To modify settings for other graph characteristics, press F10 (Menu) to display the Graph Design menu.

**5.**   Modify additional graph settings as described in the following sections.

**6.**   Press F2 (Do-It!) or press F10 (Menu) and select Do-It! to save the new graph settings. To cancel the modifications, press F10 (Menu) and select Cancel.

## THE GRAPH DESIGN MENU

While modifying a graph, you can press F10 (Menu) to display the Graph Design menu. The menu options are:

**Type:** Modifies the graph type and creates a combination graph (displays the Customize Graph Type form again)

**Overall:** Modifies graph titles, colors, axes, grids, and page layout; selects an output device; and specifies a display period

**Series:** Modifies options for series (*y*) data

**Pies:** Modifies options for pie graphs

**ViewGraph:** Displays or prints a graph, or writes the graph to a disk file

**Help:** Accesses help for graphing

**Do-It!:** Makes the modified graph settings the current settings

**Cancel:** Cancels the modifications made to the graph settings

## To Modify Graph Characteristics

Select the Overall option from the Graph Design menu. Table 7.1 shows the overall graph options you can set, the form on which you set the graph options (if applicable), and the menu selections required to display the form or set an option. The various Customize Graph forms are self-explanatory and similar in layout to the Customize Graph Type form shown in Figure 7.3. The graph options you can set are displayed on the left part of the screen, with their possible settings on the right. A number or letter is associated with each graph setting. Select a setting for an option by typing the letter or number associated with it. Some options do not have a list of possible settings;

these require you to type in text (e.g., for graph titles) or numbers instead (e.g., for specifying the number of tick marks).

**Table 7.1:** Overall Menu Options

| Options | Menu Selection(s) |
|---------|-------------------|
| Customize graph, axes titles | Titles |
| Customize graph colors on-screen | Colors Screen |
| Customize printed graph colors | Colors Printer |
| Copy color settings, screen to printer | Colors Copy ScreenToPrinter |
| Copy color settings, printer to screen | Colors Copy PrinterToScreen |
| Customize axes scaling, tick marks | Axes |
| Customize graph grids, frames | Grids |
| Customize graph layout for printing | PrinterLayout |
| Output graph to printer or other device | Device Printer 1stPrinter (*or* 2ndPrinter *or* 3rdPrinter *or* 4thPrinter) |
| Select output file format | Device File CurrentPrinter (*or* EPS *or* PIC) |
| Display graph until any key is pressed | Wait KeyStroke |
| Display graph for specified time | Wait Duration |

*Note: First select Overall from the Graph Design menu to choose these menu selections*

# To Modify Series Characteristics

Select the Series option from the Graph Design menu. Table 7.2 shows the series (*y* data) characteristics you can set, the form on which you set the graph options, and the menu selections required to display the form.

**Table 7.2**: Series Menu Options

| Options | Menu Selection |
|---|---|
| Customize series legends | LegendsAndLabels |
| Customize markers, fills | MarkersAndFills |
| *Note: First select Series from the Graph Design menu to choose these menu selections* | |

# To Modify Pie Graphs

Select the Pies option from the Graph Design menu. These settings are made on the Customize Pie Graph form and include formats for displaying pie values, selecting which pie slices to explode, and patterns and colors to use for pie slices.

# To Create a Graph
# while Modifying Current Graph Settings

1.  From the Graph mode, press F10 (Menu) to display the Graph Modify menu; select ViewGraph. Alternatively, press Ctrl–F7 (Instant Graph).

2.  Select Screen, Printer, or File to display the graph on the screen, output it, or write the graph to a disk file, respectively.

**What For?**    While you are modifying graph settings, it is often helpful to preview the effects of your settings without having to save them permanently.

## To Save the Current Graph Settings

1.  From the Main mode, press F10 (Menu) and select Image Graph Save.

2.  Enter a name for the graph file. Paradox will automatically add the extension .G to the file name you provide.

## To Recall Previously Saved Graph Settings

1.  From the Main mode, press F10 (Menu) and select Image Graph Load.

2.  Enter the name of the graph-settings file or press Enter and select from a list of graph-settings files in the current directory.

## To Reset the Current Graph Settings to Their Defaults

From the Main mode, press F10 (Menu) and select Image Graph Reset.

**See Also**    *The Custom Configuration Program* (Chapter 1) to change the default graph settings.

## *Chapter Eight*

# PARADOX TOOLS

This chapter covers most of the tools that provide support for tasks you are performing in Paradox.

# RENAMING OBJECTS

## To Rename a Paradox Object

1.  From the Main mode, press F10 (Menu) and select Tools Rename.

2.  Select the type of object you want to rename.

3.  Enter the name of the table, graph, or script (or the table that owns the form or report) you want to rename, or press Enter and select from the menu of tables, scripts, or graphs in the current directory.

4.  If you are renaming a table, script, or graph, enter the new name for this object. You are now done. If you are renaming a form or report, select its form or report number.

5.  To complete the renaming of the form or report, give it a new number.

**What For?**   The Rename tool is used to change the file name for tables, scripts, and graph settings as well as change the assigned number for existing forms and reports.

# IMPORTING AND EXPORTING

## To Import a File

1.  From the Main mode, press F10 (Menu) and select Tools ExportImport Import.

2.  Select the type of file to import.

3. Provide a name for the table that Paradox imports. If you select ASCII AppendDelimited, this must be an existing table that has a structure compatible with the delimited ASCII file.

## To Export a Table

1. From the Main mode, press F10 (Menu) and select Tools ExportImport Export.

2. Select the type of file to create from the table.

3. Enter the name of the table you want to export or press Enter to select from a menu of tables in the current directory.

4. Enter the name of the file to which you are exporting the table's data.

● **NOTE** The formats supported for these operations include Quattro and Quattro Pro, Lotus 1-2-3 (release 1A or 2), Lotus Symphony (1.0 or 1.1), dBASE (II, III, III+, or IV), PFS or IBM filing assistant, Reflex (1.0 or 1.1), VisiCalc, and ASCII (delimited or text).

**See Also** *Outputting a Report* (Chapter 5) for information on printing a report to a file.

# COPYING AND DELETING OBJECTS

## To Copy an Object

1. From the Main mode, press F10 (Menu) and select Tools Copy.

2. Select the type of object you want to copy.

3. Follow the displayed prompts to copy the object.

**What For?**   To make copies of tables, forms, reports, scripts, graph settings, or even a table's entire family (forms, reports, Val-Checks, and image settings). When you are copying a form or report, you have the option of either copying it to a different number for the same table, or to another similarly structured table.

## To Delete an Object

1.   From the Main mode, press F10 (Menu) and select Tools Delete.

2.   Select the type of object you want to delete.

3.   Follow the displayed prompts to delete the selected object.

**What For?**   To delete any of the following objects: a table and its family, a form, a report, a script, a query speedup, an image setting, a table's ValChecks, or a graph setting.

# VIEWING THE PARADOX ENVIRONMENT

The Info selection from the Tools menu allows you to display information about tables, files on a directory, locks placed on a table when you are working on a network, and other users currently running Paradox on your network. The requested information is placed in a temporary table that is displayed on the workspace.

## To Display a Table's Structure

1.   From the Main mode, press F10 (Menu) and select Tools Info Structure.

2.   Enter the name of the table whose structure you want to display or press Enter and select from a menu of tables in the current directory.

**What For?**   The Structure menu selection allows you to display the structure of a table without using Modify Restructure. This capability is one of the more useful Info tools, because knowing a table's structure is important for designing forms and reports, constructing queries, and applying ValChecks.

## To Create an Inventory List

1. From the Main mode, press F10 (Menu) and select Tools Info Inventory.

2. Select whether you want to list all tables, scripts (including saved queries), or (DOS) files.

3. Enter the path of the directory that contains the elements you want to list. To display the elements from the current directory, press Enter without specifying a path. If you selected Files in Step 2, you can also use DOS wildcard characters (* or ?) to display only those files with specific characteristics.

## To Display a Table's Family

1. From the Main Mode, press F10 (Menu) and select Tools Info Family.

2. Enter the name of the table whose family you want to display or press Enter to select from a menu of tables in the current directory.

**What For?**   Viewing a table's family displays each of the file types associated with a single table. These files include any form and report files, indices, locks, settings, and ValChecks, if present.

## To List Other Paradox Users on a Network

From the Main mode, press F10 (Menu) and select Tools Info Who.

## To List the Locks on a Table

1. From the Main mode, press F10 (Menu) and select Tools Info Lock.

2. Enter the name of the table or press Enter to select from a menu of tables in the current directory.

**What For?** When you are using Paradox on a local area network (LAN), locks are frequently placed on tables or their family members in order to either restrict other users' access to a table or ensure that a specific user maintains access to a table. When you view table locks, Paradox displays all locks that have been placed on a particular table, or that table's family.

# ADDING, SUBTRACTING, AND EMPTYING TABLES

## To Add Records from One Table to Another

1. From the Main mode, press F10 (Menu) and select Tools More Add.

2. Enter the name of the table that contains the records you want to add to another table, or press Enter to select this table from a menu of tables in the current directory.

3. Enter the name of the table to which you want to add the records or press Enter and select from a menu of tables in the current directory.

● **NOTE** The two tables must have compatible structures—i.e., their field types must match field-for-field.

## To Use MultiAdd

**1.** From the Main mode, press F10 (Menu) and select Tools More MultiAdd.

**2.** Enter the name of the source table you want to add to the table(s) or press Enter and make your selection from the menu of tables in the current directory.

**3.** Enter the name of the MultiEntry map table or press Enter to select it from the menu of tables in the current directory.

**4.** Select NewEntries to add records to the existing table(s) without replacing existing records, or Update to update existing records in the table(s) to which the new records are being added.

**What For?**   On occasion you may want to add a single table to two or more related tables. This makes sense when you have a table that contains redundant information and you already have two or more related tables that can store this information. This most often occurs when you regularly import data from a non-relational source, or when you save the Entry table created by the MultiEntry feature. In order to use MultiAdd, you must have previously defined a Multi-Entry setup (see Chapter 3).

**● NOTE**   The NewEntries option is appropriate when one or more of the tables that records are being added to are keyed. Records will not be added if they conflict with key fields in the existing tables (meaning that they duplicate existing records in key-field values). Instead, they will be placed into the temporary table called Keyviol. When the Update option is selected, and one or more tables that the data are being added to are keyed, Paradox updates the records in the tables in all cases where the key fields match.

## To Use FormAdd

**1.** From the Main mode, press F10 (Menu) and select Tools More FormAdd.

**2.** Enter the name of the master table that owns the multi-table form.

3. Select the multi-table form number.

4. Select EntryTables to add records from Entry, Entry1, Entry2, etc., or AnyTables to explicitly name the tables to add.

5. Select whether the added records are NewEntries or Update entries.

6. If you selected AnyTables in Step 4, enter the name of each table that corresponds to the multi-table form tables. (Paradox will prompt you to specify each of these tables separately.) Instead of entering these names, you can press Enter and select them from a menu of tables in the current directory.

**What For?**   FormAdd is used to add only those records from two or more tables that are related to each other, based on one or more fields. A multi-table form is used to define these relationships. This feature is particularly useful when you have entered data in an Entry table with a multi-table form and selected KeepEntry. During this process, Paradox saves the master-table data in a temporary table called Entry, and saves each of the embedded tables as Entry1, Entry2, and so on.

● **NOTE**   NewEntries and Update work the same with FormAdd as with MultiAdd, but with one important difference. If you select NewEntries and key violations are encountered, Paradox will create more than one temporary Keyviol table (named Keyviol, Keyviol1, Keyviol2, etc.) corresponding to each of the tables being added. Furthermore, Paradox will also create a temporary table called List which defines which multi-table form-tables correspond to each of the Keyviol tables.

## To Delete One Table's Records From Another

1. From the Main mode, press F10 (Menu) and select Tools More Subtract.

2. Enter the name of the table that contains the records you want to delete from the target table, or press Enter to select from a menu of tables in the current directory.

3.  Enter the name of the target table or press Enter to select from a menu of tables in the current directory.

**What For?**   Use the Subtract feature to delete one table's records (the source table) from another table (the target table). This feature can be used with both keyed and unkeyed tables. When you use this feature with keyed tables, Paradox deletes all records from the target table that match source-table records based on the key-field values. When you use this feature on unkeyed tables, only those records in the target table that exactly match source-table records are deleted.

## To Empty a Table

1.  From the Main mode, press F10 (Menu) and select Tools More Empty.

2.  Enter the name of the table you want to empty or press Enter and select from a menu of tables in the current directory.

3.  Select Ok.

# PASSWORD PROTECTION

You can define a master password for any table or script (including saved queries) to prevent unauthorized entry. (Password-protected scripts can be played without having to provide a password, but they cannot be changed.) In addition, password-protected tables and scripts are encrypted so that anyone who views them on a word processor, file-viewing utility, or by any other method, will only see a string of jumbled characters.

The first time you attempt to access a table or script that is password protected, Paradox will ask you to enter a password. If you enter a valid password, all tables or scripts that are protected by that password will become available to you for the rest of your Paradox session, or until you clear the passwords.

## To Protect a Table or Script

**1.** From the Main mode, press F10 (Menu) and select Tools More Protect Password.

**2.** Select whether to protect a table or a script.

**3.** Enter the name of the table or script, or press Enter and select what you want from the menu.

**4.** If the table or script is already protected, Paradox will require you to enter the master password before continuing.

**5.** Enter the new master password. A password is case-sensitive (i.e., capitalization matters); it may also be up to 15 characters long and may include spaces.

**6.** Verify the password by entering it a second time.

**7.** If you are protecting a script, it will become encrypted. If you are protecting a table, you will enter the Password mode and see the auxiliary-password form shown in Figure 8.1. If you do not want to enter auxiliary passwords, or when you are through defining them, press F2 (Do-It!).

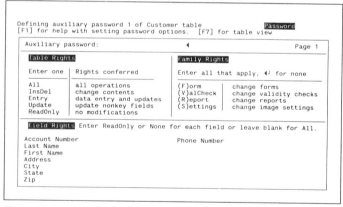

**Figure 8.1:** The Auxiliary-password form

## To Assign Auxiliary Password(s)

**1.** From the Password mode, enter the password next to the Auxiliary password prompt on the auxiliary-password form shown in Figure 8.1. The auxiliary password is case-sensitive, may be up to 15 characters long, and may include spaces.

**2.** Optionally, assign table rights, family rights, and field rights to the password.

**3.** To define another password for the table, press the Page Down key and repeat Steps 1 and 2.

**4.** Press F2 (Do-It!) when you are finished.

**What For?** After you have defined or verified the master password for a table, you have the option of defining one or more auxiliary passwords. Auxiliary passwords grant other users access to a table without them needing to know the master password. You can assign as many auxiliary passwords as you like to a single table. Likewise, you can assign the same auxiliary password to as many tables as you like so that authorized users need only remember a single password.

When you define an auxiliary password, you define exactly what kind of access that password allows. For example, one auxiliary password may permit users to do anything to a table except change the master password (the least restrictive type), while another may restrict a user to view merely one field in a table. Typically, auxiliary passwords provide users with privileges somewhere between these two extremes.

The Table Rights option permits you to specify what type of operation the auxiliary password permits. If you leave this option blank, it will default to All. To restrict the table rights provided by the auxiliary password, enter the first letter of the desired table-rights option from the list displayed.

The Family Rights option is used to define which types of changes the password allows to a table's family. If you leave this option blank, the auxiliary password will permit no changes to any of the table's family. To permit changes, enter the first letter for each of the family objects that can be changed from the list displayed below the option.

The area labeled Field Rights at the bottom of the form displays each field from the table. If desired, you may permit only certain operations on specific fields. To restrict access to any field, move the cursor to the position to the immediate right of the field name and enter **R** (ReadOnly) or **N** (None).

## To Clear All Passwords

From the Main mode, press F10 (Menu) and select Tools More Protect ClearPasswords.

**What For?**   To revoke (clear) entered passwords during your Paradox session. This is useful when you need to leave your computer unattended and you do not want to leave your tables and/or scripts unprotected. After clearing your passwords, you will be required to provide a password again before being able to access any protected tables or scripts.

## To Remove a Master Password

1.   From the Main mode press F10 (Menu) and select Tools More Protect Password.

2.   Enter the name of the table from which you want to remove the passwords or press Enter and select from a menu of tables in the current directory.

3.   Enter the current master password.

4.   Select Master.

5.   Press Enter to remove the master password and all auxiliary passwords.

## To Add, Change, or Delete an Auxiliary Password

1.  From the Main menu press F10 (Menu) and select Tools More Protect Password.

2.  Enter the name of the table or press Enter and select from a menu of tables in the current directory.

3.  Enter the current master password.

4.  Select Auxiliary.

5.  To add a new password, press Ins. To change or delete an existing password, use the Page Up and Page Down keys until the desired auxiliary password is displayed in the Auxiliary-password field.

6.  Define the new auxiliary-password rights or make changes to the existing rights, or press the Del key to delete the auxiliary password.

7.  To add, change, or delete any additional auxiliary passwords, repeat Steps 5 and 6.

8.  Press F2 (Do-It!) when you are finished.

## To Add or Remove Write-protection for a Table

1.  From the Main mode, press F10 (Menu) and select Tools More Protect Write-protect.

2.  Enter the name of the table you want to write-protect or press Enter to select from a menu of tables in the current directory.

3.  To write-protect the table, select Set. To remove Write-protection, select Clear.

**What For?**   Write-protection is used to prevent accidental changes to tables. When a table is write-protected, no one may make changes to it, although they may view the table and even query it. As long as a table is not password protected, anyone may write-protect a table or remove write-protection from a table.

# CHANGING DIRECTORIES

## To Change Your Current Directory

1. From the Main mode, press F10 (Menu) and select Tools More Directory.

2. Enter the name of a new directory.

3. Select Ok.

● **NOTE** When you change the current directory, Paradox removes all images from the workspace and deletes all temporary tables. If you have any temporary tables that you do not want to lose, rename them before you change directories.

# ACCESSING DOS WITHIN PARADOX

## To Temporarily Exit to DOS

1. From the Main mode, press F10 (Menu) and select Tools More ToDOS. Alternatively, press Ctrl–O (DOS) or Alt–O (Big DOS).

2. Enter **EXIT** to exit DOS and return to Paradox.

● **NOTE** ToDOS and Ctrl–O (DOS) both provide you with at least 140K of memory. Alt–O (Big DOS) provides closer to 500K.

Whichever method you use to exit to DOS temporarily, you should observe these two rules:

- Do not delete any Paradox objects while in DOS. This may cause Paradox to crash upon your return from DOS

- Do not turn off your computer without returning to Paradox and using the Main menu selection Exit

## Chapter Nine

# SCRIPTS

Scripts contain instructions that Paradox can read. The instructions tell Paradox what to do and how to do it. Some scripts are full-fledged computer programs, while others are more similar to keyboard macros that contain a series of keystrokes that you previously entered.

# CREATING SCRIPTS

## To Begin Creating a Recorded Script

1. From the Main mode, press F10 (Menu) and select Scripts BeginRecord. Alternatively, press Alt–F10 (PAL Menu) and select BeginRecord from any mode.

2. Enter a name for the script you want to begin recording.

**What For?**   A recorded script is used to store a sequence of keystrokes. When you play it, the keystrokes are entered again, just as if you were entering them manually. Recorded scripts are ideal for recording tasks you perform on an occasional basis. .

## To Finish a Recorded Script

From the Main mode, press F10 (Menu) and select Scripts End-Record. Alternatively, press Alt–F10 (PAL Menu) and select EndRecord from any mode.

## To Create an Instant Script

Press Alt–F3 from any mode. This is a toggle; press Alt–F3 to finish recording.

**What For?**   An instant script is similar to a recorded script. However, Paradox allows only one instant script to exist at a time, called INSTANT.SC. It is ideal for repeating a task many times in a row.

# PLAYING SCRIPTS

## To Play a Recorded Script

1.  From the Main mode, press F10 (Menu) and select Scripts Play. Alternatively, press Alt–F10 (PAL Menu) and select Play from any mode.

2.  Enter the name of the script you want to play or press Enter and select from the menu of scripts in the current directory.

● **NOTE**   If something goes wrong (e.g., the mode in which the script was created differs from the mode in which you play the script), Paradox will show you a menu with two selections, Cancel and Debug. Select Cancel to stop playing the script and solve the problem (e.g., enter the correct mode) before playing the script again.

## To Play an Instant Script

Press Alt–F4 from any mode.

● **NOTE**   Alt–F4 plays any script named INSTANT.SC, whether it was created as an instant script or a recorded script (and later renamed INSTANT.SC).

## To Use ShowPlay

1.  From the Main mode, press F10 (Menu) and select Scripts ShowPlay.

2.  Enter the name of the script you want to play or press Enter and select from the menu of scripts in the current directory.

3. Select Fast or Slow to determine the speed at which the script is played.

**What For?** ShowPlay allows you to play a script and observe how it functions "behind the scenes." When you play a script, the screen appears to be frozen; this is actually the PAL canvas. When you select ShowPlay, the PAL canvas becomes "transparent" while the script is playing, allowing you to see the effects of each keystroke. The ShowPlay feature is best used with recorded scripts created in the Main mode.

● **NOTE** You cannot ShowPlay an encrypted script unless you first enter the script's password.

## To Play a Script Repeatedly

1. From the Main mode, press F10 (Menu) and select Scripts RepeatPlay.

2. Enter the name of the script to play or press Enter and select from the menu of scripts in the current directory.

3. Indicate how many times you want to play the script.

# QUERYSAVE

QuerySave is used to store a query on the workspace as a script. An example of a script containing a saved query is shown in Figure 9.1. Using QuerySave, you can instantly regenerate a query by playing the script that contains it.

## To Save a Query for Future Use

1. With the desired query displayed, press F10 (Menu) from the Main mode and select Scripts QuerySave.

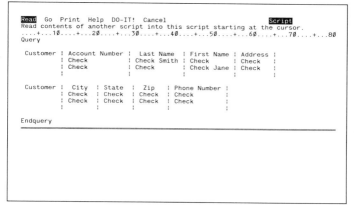

```
 Read  Go  Print  Help  DO-IT!  Cancel                        Script
 Read contents of another script into this script starting at the cursor.
....+...10....+...20....+...30....+...40....+...50....+...60....+...70....+...80
 Query

 Customer ¦ Account Number ¦  Last Name ¦ First Name ¦ Address ¦
          ¦ Check          ¦ Check Smith ¦ Check     ¦ Check   ¦
          ¦ Check          ¦ Check       ¦ Check Jane ¦ Check  ¦
          ¦                ¦             ¦           ¦         ¦

 Customer ¦  City ¦ State ¦  Zip  ¦ Phone Number ¦
          ¦ Check ¦ Check ¦ Check ¦ Check        ¦
          ¦ Check ¦ Check ¦ Check ¦ Check        ¦
          ¦       ¦       ¦       ¦              ¦

 Endquery
```

**Figure 9.1:** A script containing a saved query

2. Enter a name for the saved query. This name can be up to eight characters long. To replace an existing saved query (script) with the current query, enter the name of that script.

## To Use a Saved Query

1. Remove any query forms currently on the workspace by (a) making them current using the F3 (Up Image) and F4 (Down Image) keys and (b) pressing F8 (Clear Image).

2. Press F10 (Menu) from the Main mode and select Scripts Play.

3. Enter the name of the script that contains the saved query, or press Enter and select from the menu of scripts in the current directory. Paradox will re-create the query on the workspace.

4. If desired, make changes to the displayed query.

5. Press F2 (Do-It!) to initiate the query.

# THE PAL EDITOR

The PAL editor is an ASCII text editor that is built into Paradox. Figure 9.1 shows the PAL editor screen containing a query saved as a script.

## To Access the PAL Editor

1. From any mode except Scripts, press F10 (Menu) and select Scripts Editor.

2. To write a new script with PAL, select Write. To change an existing script, select Edit.

## To Display the PAL Editor Menu

From Scripts mode, press F10 (Menu).

The PAL Editor Menu contains the following menu options:

**Read:** Inserts an existing script, starting below the line the cursor is currently on

**Go:** Saves and plays the current script

**Do-It!:** Saves the current script and returns to the Paradox menu

**Cancel:** Exits the current script without saving it and returns to the Main menu

Table 9.1 shows the keys you can use while working in the PAL Editor.

**Table 9.1**: Keys Used in the PAL Editor

| Key | Effect |
|---|---|
| Backspace | Deletes character to the left of the cursor |
| Ctrl–End | Moves cursor to the end of the line |
| Ctrl–Home | Moves cursor to the beginning of the current line |
| Ctrl– ← | Moves script left one screen |
| Ctrl– → | Moves script right one screen |
| Ctrl–V | Displays Vertical rule |
| Ctrl–Y | Deletes all characters to the right of the cursor |
| Del | Deletes character at the cursor |
| ↓ | Moves cursor down one line |
| → | Moves cursor to the right |
| ↑ | Moves cursor up one line |
| ← | Moves cursor to the left |
| End | Moves cursor to the last line in the script |
| Enter | In insert mode, inserts a new line; in typeover mode, moves down one line |
| Home | Moves cursor to the first line in the script |
| Ins | Toggles between insert and typeover modes |
| Page Down | Moves cursor down one half-screen |
| Page Up | Moves cursor up one half-screen |

## Chapter Ten

# PARADOX ON A NETWORK

This chapter describes Paradox's network features, including locks, user names, private tables and directories, and the screen-refresh cycle.

Paradox databases are network-ready. That is, Paradox manages and resolves competition for network resources, permitting two or more people to use the same Paradox objects simultaneously. When many people are using Paradox on a network, they all have the ability to view, edit, report, and query any tables stored in a shared directory (a directory to which each user has access). Some types of access, however, require rights that are incompatible with other types of access. For instance, if one user is performing an insert query, no other users may access that table in any way.

# LOCKED TABLES

Paradox manages competition for access to Paradox objects through the use of *locks.* When you need sole access to a table, Paradox automatically places one or more locks on it. While these locks do not affect *your* use of the table, these locks restrict the access of other users to it.

When you attempt to use a Paradox object, Paradox first checks whether or not any other users currently have a lock on the object that would prohibit your access. If such a lock exists, Paradox will deny you access and display a message identifying the user who has placed the restricting lock.

There are five types of locks, shown in Table 10.1.

## To Lock a Table

1.  From the Main mode, press F10 (Menu) and select Tools Net.

**Table 10.1**: Types of Table Locks

| Lock | Effect |
|------|--------|
| Full lock | No other user may access the table |
| Write lock | No other user may write to the table |
| Prevent-write lock | No other user may place a write lock on the table |
| Prevent-full lock | No other user may place a full lock on the table |
| Form lock | No other user may use the table except through the current multi-table form |

**2.** Select the type of lock you want to place. To place a write or full lock on a table, select Lock. To place a prevent-write or prevent-full lock on a table, select PreventLock.

**3.** Select FullLock or WriteLock, depending on the type of Lock or PreventLock you place.

**4.** Enter the name of the table you want to lock, or press Enter and select from the menu of tables in the current directory.

**What For?** Although Paradox automatically places locks on tables based on the Paradox operations you are performing, you can also manually place and remove them. This capability is particularly important if you need to ensure that you have a particular level of access to one or more tables. For instance, if you are preparing to print a report, you may want to place a write lock on the report table manually, rather than take a chance that the table will be available at the instant you begin printing the report.

• **NOTE** A form lock cannot be placed manually. Form locks occur automatically only when one user accesses a table with a multi-table form. While the form lock is in place, multiple users may access the master table and detail table(s) through the multi-table form only.

# PRIVATE DIRECTORIES AND PRIVATE TABLES

## To Change Your Private Directory

**1.** From the Main mode, press F10 (Menu) and select Tools Net SetPrivate.

**2.** Enter the path of your private directory.

**3.** Select Ok.

**What For?** On a network, every user has a private directory where Paradox stores temporary tables and other temporary objects. The intent of this is to prevent competition between two or more users for tables such as the Answer table from a query. (Otherwise, one user's query might replace another user's Answer table.) In some situations, however, a task you perform may require an inordinate amount of network resources and bog down other users. Therefore you would want to reassign your private directory to a local hard disk to reduce your use of the network.

● **NOTE** Changing your private directory will cause Paradox to delete all temporary tables stored in it.

# USERNAME

## To Change Your User Name

1. From the Main mode, press F10 (Menu) and select Tools Net UserName.

2. Enter a new user name. Your user name may contain up to 14 characters.

3. Select Ok.

This name change lasts only for the duration of your Paradox session.

**What For?** Your user name identifies you to Paradox and other Paradox users on the network. You can change it to one that is more meaningful, such as your last name.

● **NOTE** Use the Custom Configuration Program to change your private directory or user name permanently.

# AUTOREFRESH

When multiple users are making changes to the same table simultaneously (with CoEdit), all users who are viewing the particular records being changed will see these changes as they are made. This is because Paradox updates the display image of the table at regular intervals. The length of the interval is called the *refresh period*. The default refresh-period is defined with the Custom Configuration Program: when Paradox is installed, this period is set to three seconds.

## To Change the Refresh Period

1. From the Main mode, press F10 (Menu) and select Tools Net AutoRefresh.

2. Enter the number of seconds for the new refresh period.

This refresh-period change lasts only for the duration of your Paradox session.

**What For?**   When you need to always have the most current table data displayed, set your refresh period to a short interval. If the accuracy of the data is not critical, a longer refresh period will provide you with a less active and distracting view of your data.

*Appendix A*

# PAL FUNCTIONS AND FORMAT SPECIFIERS

# PAL FUNCTIONS IN FORMS AND REPORTS

Table A.1 contains a complete list of all PAL (Paradox Application Language) functions that can be used in forms and reports. You use these functions by entering them into a calculated field. See Chapters 4 and 5 for information on placing calculated fields in forms and reports.

**Table A.1:** PAL Functions for Forms and Reports

| Function | Type of Value Returned | Effect |
|---|---|---|
| ABS(*n*) | N | Returns the absolute value of *n* |
| ACOS(*n*) | N | Returns the arc cosine of *n* |
| ASC (*character*) | N | Converts *character* to an ASCII value |
| ASIN(*n*) | N | Returns the arc sine of *n* |
| ATAN(*n*) | N | Returns the arc tangent of *n* |
| ATAN2(*n*) | N | Returns the four quadrant arc tangent of *n* |
| CAVERAGE (*tablename, fieldname*) | N | Returns the average of values in the *fieldname* column |
| CCOUNT (*tablename, fieldname*) | N | Returns the number of values in the *fieldname* column |
| CHR(*n*) | A1 | Converts the ASCII *n* to a character |
| CMAX (*tablename, fieldname*) | N | Returns the largest value in the *fieldname* column |

**Table A.1:** PAL Functions for Forms and Reports (continued)

| Function | Type of Value Returned | Effect |
|---|---|---|
| CMIN (*tablename, fieldname*) | N | Returns the smallest value in the *fieldname* column |
| CNPV (*tablename, fieldname, n*) | N | Returns the net present value of the *fieldname* column using the interest rate or discount (in decimal format) specified by *n* |
| COS(*n*) | N | Returns the cosine of *n* |
| CSTD (*tablename, fieldname*) | N | Returns the standard deviation of the values in the *fieldname* column |
| CSUM (*tablename, fieldname*) | N | Returns the sum of the values in the *fieldname* column |
| CVAR (*tablename, fieldname*) | N | Returns the variance of the values in the *fieldname* column |
| DATEVAL (*string*) | D | Converts *string* to a date |
| DAY(*date*) | N | Returns day of the *date* as a number |
| DOW(*date*) | A3 | Returns a three-letter abbreviation of the day of the week of *date* |
| EXP(*n*) | N | Returns the base-*e* exponent of *n* |
| FILL (*character, n*) | A | Returns *n* repetitions of *character* |
| FORMAT (*format, string*) | A | Formats *string* using the *format* specified (see Table A.2) |

**Table A.1:** PAL Functions for Forms and Reports (continued)

| Function | Type of Value Returned | Effect |
|---|---|---|
| FV (*n1*, *n2*, *n3*) | N | Returns future value of payments (*n1* = payment value, *n2* = interest rate period, *n3* = number of periods) |
| INT(*n*) | N | Returns *n* as an integer |
| LEN (*expression*) | N | Returns the length of *expression* |
| LN(*n*) | N | Returns the natural log of *n* |
| LOG(*n*) | N | Returns the base-10 log of *n* |
| LOWER (*expression*) | A | Returns *expression* in lowercase |
| MAX (*n1*, *n2*) | N | Returns the larger of *n1* and *n2* |
| MIN (*n1*, *n2*) | N | Returns the smaller of *n1* and *n2* |
| MOD (*n1*, *n2*) | N | Returns the remainder of *n1* / *n2* |
| MONTH (*date*) | N | Returns month of the *date* as a number |
| MOY(*date*) | A3 | Returns the three-letter abbreviation of the month of *date* |
| NRECORDS (*tablename*) | N | Returns the number of records in *tablename* |
| NUMVAL (*string*) | N | Converts *string* to a number |
| PI( ) | N | Returns $\pi$ |
| PMT (*n1*, *n2*, *n3*) | N | Returns amortized mortgage payments (*n1* = loan principal, *n2* = interest rate period, *n3* = number of periods) |
| POW (*n1*, *n2*) | N | Returns *n1* raised to the *n2* power |

**Table A.1:** PAL Functions for Forms and Reports (continued)

| Function | Type of Value Returned | Effect |
|---|---|---|
| PV (*n1*, *n2*, *n3*) | N | Returns the present value of payments (*n1* = payment period, *n2* = interest rate period, *n3* = number of periods) |
| RAND( ) | N | Returns a random number between 0 and 1 |
| ROUND (*n1*, *n2*) | N | Rounds *n1* to *n2* decimal places |
| SEARCH (*substring*, *string*) | N | Returns the position of *substring* in *string* |
| SIN(*n*) | N | Returns the sine of *n* |
| SQRT(*n*) | N | Returns the square root of *n* |
| STRVAL (*expression*) | A | Converts *expression* value to a string |
| SUBSTR (*string*, *n1*, *n2*) | A | Returns part of *string* that is *n2* characters long, beginning with the *n1st* position |
| TAN(*n*) | N | Returns the tangent of *n* in radians |
| TIME( ) | A | Returns present time in 24-hour format |
| TODAY( ) | D | Returns today's date |
| UPPER (*string*) | A | Returns *expression* in uppercase |
| USERNAME ( ) | A | Returns your current user's name |
| YEAR(*date*) | N | Returns year of the *date* as a number |

# FORMAT SPECIFIERS

Table A.2 contains the various format specifiers that you use with the FORMAT function. A specifier must be enclosed in quotes; two or more specifiers must be separated by a comma. For instance, to center data from a table's *Last Name* field in a 20-character-wide region, you would type

FORMAT ("W20, AC", [Last Name])

**Table A.2:** Format Function Specifiers

| Format Specifier | Applies to Value Type | Effect |
|---|---|---|
| **Width:** | | |
| W*n* | All | Allowable width of *n* |
| W*n.m* | N, $ | Width of *n* to *m* decimal places |
| **Alignment:** | | |
| AC | All | Aligns center |
| AL | All | Aligns left |
| AR | All | Aligns right |
| **Case:** | | |
| CC | All | Capitalizes initial letters |
| CL | All | Lowercases all letters |
| CU | All | Uppercases all letters |
| **Edit:** | | |
| E$ | N, S, $ | Floating dollar sign ($) |
| E* | N, S, $ | Uses asterisks (*) for leading zeros |

**Table A.2**: Format Function Specifiers (continued)

| Format Specifier | Applies to Value Type | Effect |
| --- | --- | --- |
| EB | N, S, $ | Uses blanks for leading zeros |
| EC | N, S, $ | Inserts whole number separators |
| EI | N, S, $ | Uses international notation |
| ES | N, S, $ | Uses scientific notation |
| EZ | N, S, $ | Uses leading zeros |
| **Sign:** | | |
| S+ | N, S, $ | Shows leading plus or minus (+ or −) sign |
| S− | N, S, $ | Shows leading minus (−) sign |
| SC | N, S, $ | Suffixes negative values with CR |
| SD | N, S, $ | Uses DB/CR notation |
| SP | N, S, $ | Uses parentheses for negative values |
| **Date:** | | |
| D1 | D | Uses *mm/dd/yy* format |
| D2 | D | Uses *Month/dd/yyyy* format |
| D3 | D | Uses *mm/dd* format |
| D4 | D | Uses *mm/yy* format |
| D5 | D | Uses *dd–Mon–yy* format |
| D6 | D | Uses *Mon yy* format |
| D7 | D | Uses *dd–Mon–yyyy* format |
| D8 | D | Uses *mm/dd/yyyy* format |
| D9 | D | Uses *dd.mm.yy* format |

**Table A.2:** Format Function Specifiers (continued)

| Format Specifier | Applies to Value Type | Effect |
|---|---|---|
| D10 | D | Uses $dd/mm/yy$ format |
| D11 | D | Uses $yy–mm–dd$ format |
| **Logical:** | | |
| LO | L | Uses On/Off instead of True/False |
| LY | L | Uses Yes/No instead of True/False |

*Appendix B*

# THE PARADOX SQL LINK

The Paradox SQL Link is an add-on product of Borland International that works in conjunction with Paradox 3.5. It permits you to access tables residing on a *database server*—a computer specifically designed to support database operations. The advantage of the Paradox SQL Link is that you can use familiar Paradox features to access data on a database server.

Version 1.0 of the SQL Link permits access to three different database servers. More servers will be added in future versions. The servers that are currently supported are:

- IBM Extended Edition 1.2 Database Manager

- Microsoft SQL Server 1.0 or later

- ORACLE Server 6.0 or later

Before you can access the database server data using the SQL Link, you must connect it to the server. There are several ways to do this, depending on the requirement of your server. At a minimum, this process entails providing your user name and user password to the server. The connection to the server is made by pressing F10 from the Main mode and selecting Tools SQL Connection Select.

Upon connecting to a server, Paradox creates local versions of each of the tables on the server that you want to access. (Local tables are Paradox tables; remote tables are SQL tables.) The local versions of remote tables are called *replicas*. Replicas are not exact duplicates of remote tables; rather, they are empty local Paradox tables. Using the replicas, you can design forms and reports for remote tables, query remote tables, and even add or update data to remote tables. Furthermore, you can copy, delete, and empty remote tables, as well as apply password protection.

# *Index*

# Function Keys

| Function Key | Key Name |
|---|---|
| F1 | Help |
| F2 | Do-It! |
| Alt–F2 | Show SQL |
| F3 | Up Image |
| Alt–F3 | Instant Script Record Toggle |
| F4 | Down Image |
| Alt–F4 | Instant Script Play |
| F5 | Example |
| Alt–F5 | Field View |
| F6 | Check |
| Alt–F6 | Check Plus |
| Ctrl–F6 | Check Descending |
| Shift–F6 | Group |
| F7 | Form Toggle |
| Alt–F7 | Instant Report |
| Ctrl–F7 | Graph |
| F8 | Clear Image |
| Alt–F8 | Clear All |
| F9 | Edit |
| Alt–F9 | CoEdit |
| F10 | Menu |
| Ctrl–F10 | Quattro Pro |